# THE CALL

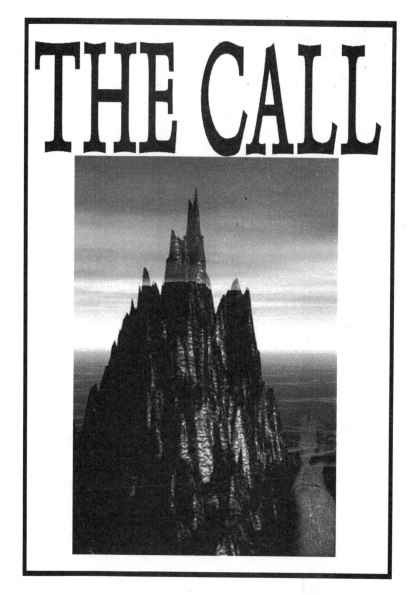

# THE CALL

# RICK JOYNER

Whitaker House

Unless otherwise stated, all Scripture quotations are taken from the *New American Standard Bible*, (NAS) © 1960, 1962, 1968, 1971, 1973, 1975, 1977 by The Lockman Foundation. Used by permission.

Italics in Scripture references are for emphasis only.

## THE CALL

Rick Joyner
MorningStar Publications
303 Hollywood Road
Moravian Falls, NC 28654
1.800.542.0278
Fax: 1.336.838.6380

ISBN: 0-88368-602-3
Printed in the United States of America
Copyright © 1999 by Rick Joyner
Cover art and design by Dianne C. Thomas

Whitaker House
30 Hunt Valley Circle
New Kensington, PA 15068

Library of Congress Cataloging-in-Publication Data

Joyner, Rick, 1949–
    The call / by Rick Joyner.
        p.   cm.
    Sequel to: The final quest.
    Originally published: Charlotte, NC : MorningStar Publications, c1999.
    ISBN 0-88368-602-3 (trade paper : alk. paper)
    1. End of the world. 2. Private revelations. I. Title

BT876.J69 2000
248.2'9—dc21                                         99-059144

2  3  4  5  6  7  8  9  10  11  12 / 09  08  07  06  05  04  03  02  01  00

This book is dedicated to the Ministry Team and Staff at MorningStar Publications and Ministries. Your devotion to excellence, integrity and sacrificial service for the sake of the gospel is a great inspiration to me and is bearing fruit that will never perish.

# CONTENTS

# introduction

This is the second book in *The Final Quest* **Series.** Although *The Call* begins where the first book ends, it is possible to read this one and generally understand its message without having read the first book. However, if you have not yet read *The Final Quest*, some of the material may seem disconnected. Since this is a continuing spiritual saga, there are some foundations laid in the first book that are built upon in the second.

As I explained in the introduction to *The Final Quest*, these books are the result of a series of "prophetic experiences." Many times I have been advised that they would be received by more people if I had written them as fictional allegory. That may be true, but it is not my goal to have these books read by more people, but to simply remain faithful to the messages with which I have been entrusted, conveying them as accurately as I can. For me to claim that these are the result of my own creativity would be both dishonest and an affront to the Spirit of Truth.

Even so, because *The Final Quest* has been widely received across the spectrum of Christian denominations and movements and has found remarkable favor with conservative evangelicals, I want to explain in more depth what I mean by "prophetic experiences," how I received these in particular, and a little about the biblical basis for these experiences in our own times.

Biblical prophetic experiences are very diverse in nature, as were those which I received in this unfolding series. Some came in dreams, others in visions, and still others in what the Bible calls "trances." Dreams, visions and trances all have biblical precedents and are established ways that the Lord speaks to His people. There is such an increasing number of Christians who are having such experiences today that it is regarded by some to be a fulfillment of Peter's prophecy on the Day of Pentecost which he quoted from the prophet Joel:

> "And it shall be in the last days," God says, "That
> I will pour forth of My Spirit upon all mankind;
> and your sons and your daughters shall prophesy,
> and your young men shall see visions, and your old
> men shall dream dreams;
> Even upon My bondslaves, both men and
> women, I will in those days pour forth of My Spirit
> and they shall prophesy" (Acts 2:17-18).

As this Scripture declares, prophetic revelations through visions, dreams and prophecies will be prevalent in the last days. Because there is such a dramatic increase in revelation being given to Christians in these times, it is understandable why it is regarded as a sign that we are indeed in the "last days."

## Discerning the True From the False

Jesus also warned that in the last days there would be many **"false prophets" (Matthew 24:24).** This is to be expected because as the Lord also taught, whenever He sows wheat in a field, the enemy comes along and sows tares in the same field (Matthew 13:24-30). Tares look like wheat, and may even taste like wheat, but they are noxious. Satan will immediately try to counterfeit everything that God is doing, creating confusion and, if possible, deceiving even the elect. However, Satan could not do this if God did not allow it. Obviously the Lord wants us to learn to distinguish the real from the false and allow the real to be tested by the false in order to purify that which is true.

That false prophets are also becoming more prevalent should not surprise us, but rather encourage us to seek the real with greater determination. If we do not want to be deceived by the false, the answer is not to reject all prophecy, but rather to know what is true. Those who cannot discern true prophecy in the times to come will be increasingly subject to the false. If God is planting something, it is because we will need it. If we do not plant a field, but rather neglect it, the only harvest reaped will be weeds. Those who do not receive what God is doing today will end up reaping that which grows wild.

From the beginning, the Lord was committed to allowing mankind to choose between the real and the false, the good and the evil. That is why He put the Tree of the Knowledge of Good and Evil in the Garden along with the Tree of Life. He did not put the Tree of Knowledge there in order to cause us to stumble, but rather so that we could prove our obedience and love for Him. There can be no true obedience from the heart unless there is the freedom to disobey.

Likewise, true teachers and true teaching will always be shadowed by false teachers and false teaching; true prophets and true prophecy will always be shadowed by the false. The Lord allows the enemy to sow tares among the wheat in order to test our hearts. Those who love the truth will discern what is true, and those who are pure in heart will discern that which is pure.

That the Lord would warn us that there will be false prophets at the end of the age implies that there will be true ones, or He simply would have said that at the end of the age, all prophets will be false. Some do believe that all prophets at the end will be false, but this is a basic conflict with Joel's prophecy that at the end, God will pour out His Spirit and there will be visions, dreams and prophecy (Joel 2:28-29).

There is a danger in being open to prophetic revelations such as dreams, visions, and prophecy. However, there is a much greater danger if we are not open to them. Revelations are not given to us for our entertainment, but because we need them for the times in which we live. As Jesus also declared,

> "Truly, truly, I say to you, he who does not enter by the door into the fold of the sheep, but climbs up some other way, he is a thief and a robber.
>
> "But he who enters by the door is a shepherd of the sheep.
>
> "To him the doorkeeper opens, and the sheep hear his voice, and he calls his own sheep by name, and leads them out.
>
> "When he puts forth all his own, he goes before them, and the sheep follow him because they know his voice.
>
> "And a stranger they simply will not follow, but will flee from him, because they do not know the voice of strangers" (John 10:1-5).

The Lord's sheep know His voice. They are not deceived by strangers because they know His voice so well they can distinguish it from the voices of others. One of the ways that the Lord has spoken to His people from earliest times has been prophetically. Because we know that God never changes, and because the Scriptures are so clear about the visions, dreams, and prophecies that He will give to His people, it is imperative for us to distinguish His revelation from the enemy's and then to interpret His messages correctly. After they are interpreted correctly, we must then have the wisdom to apply them correctly.

## The Purpose of Prophecy

Prophecy is given for encouragement, but it is also given for edification. To edify means "to build." Much of my life and ministry has been built on fulfilled prophetic words. Almost every major aspect of our ministry, including the places where I go to minister or speak, are foretold prophetically. I do not consider doing something or going somewhere to minister unless the Lord has spoken to me in advance. Jesus did the same. He did not respond to human needs: He only did what He saw the Father doing. We do not have time to go places or start things that God is not leading us to do. I think that our devotion to hearing from the Lord before we do things enables us to be fruitful with the resources and time entrusted to us.

I know of others who have successfully built a ministry or church on prophetic words. I also know of some who have been shipwrecked and others who suffered serious diversions because they did not know how to judge prophecy. Many of these problems happened because they received genuine revelation from the Lord, but misinterpreted or misapplied it. For some, this may sound too complicated, but it is the process clearly established by the Scriptures, and we will pay a dear price if we deviate from sound biblical wisdom in regard to prophetic revelation.

As Jesus said in Matthew 22:29, **"Ye do err not knowing the Scriptures or the power of God"** (KJV). Many today make errors because they know the Scriptures but do not know the power of God. Those who know His power often make mistakes because they do not know the Scriptures as they should. If we are going to keep from making mistakes, we must know both the Scriptures *and* the power of God. Prophecy was never intended to replace the Bible, and the Bible was never intended to replace prophecy.

I have spent many hours with conservative evangelical leaders of major ministries to whom God has begun speaking through dreams, visions and prophecy. In many cases, He began to do this even when it violated their theology. This has become so widespread that I have begun to wonder if there are any conservative evangelical leaders with whom God is not dealing in this way. At MorningStar, there is almost a steady stream of contacts from those who are seeking help in understanding what is happening to them. What they may not understand at this point is that prophetic people also need their help every bit as much as conservative evangelicals need the help of those who have some experience with the prophetic gifts. For the church to achieve the maturity to which she is called, there must be a union between those who know the Scriptures and those who know the power of God, and this is now happening at a fast pace.

I have searched the Bible to verify that the teachings given in my experiences are biblical, and I am confident that they are. I do admit that some of them caused me to view certain Scriptures in a way that I had not previously seen them. Even so, I believe that this is consistent with the purpose of such prophetic revelations. *Prophecy should not be used to establish doctrine*. We were given the Bible for that, and I believe that the doctrine of the Bible is complete and must never be added to. However, the Bible itself has many examples of prophetic experiences given to individuals for the purpose of illuminating the Scriptures.

A prominent New Testament example of this would be the trance into which Peter fell, resulting in his trip to Cornelius' house and opening the door of faith to the Gentiles. This experience and the fruit it bore clarified for the church that the Lord also intended for the gospel to be preached to the Gentiles. This did not establish a new doctrine, but illuminated what the Scriptures said and what the Lord, Himself, had taught when He was with them, but which they apparently had forgotten.

Many of the experiences included in these two books did the same for me. They constantly reminded me of my own teachings and teachings I had heard from others, but at best had only superficially implemented in my life. In this way, these prophetic experiences were a constant challenge to me, bringing essential correction, and even judgment, to my own life and teachings. As I was the one having the experiences, I took them personally and do not presume that the same corrections are needed by everyone. However, I do believe that many of them, if not most of them, are generally applicable to the church in our time.

There are a number of recurring themes in this discourse. Not only are there repetitious statements, but some of these themes are repeated from different perspectives or worded differently in various situations. I realize that this may have been done because of my own dullness, just as it seemed that the Lord had to repeat himself over and over to Peter. I also realize that such repetition is not good literary style, but style is not my goal here. Each time something is repeated, the probability that it will be retained is increased. I have therefore tried to repeat everything just as it was repeated to me.

## Prophetic Experiences

I also understand how the nature of some of these revelations would cause theological problems for some. One of these would certainly be the way that I met and talked with many Old and New Testament characters, as well as prominent people in church history who are now dead. There are biblical precedents for this, such as when the Lord talked to Moses and Elijah. Even though Elijah was carried up without dying, Moses had died. We also have the example when the apostle John fell down to worship the angel in Revelation 22:9. The angel rebuked John, declaring that he, too, was a fellow servant of his brethren (Revelation 22:9). Many have understood this to indicate that this was one of the saints who had gone on to be with the Lord.

Even so, I can understand how some would still have a problem with this, and there is another explanation. There is a difference between prophetic experiences and actually doing something. For example, when Ezekiel was caught up in the Spirit and carried to Jerusalem, it is obvious that he was not taken to the actual Jerusalem, even though it seemed very real to him. Much of what he experienced did not actually exist, but was meant to convey a message to the exiles.

Likewise, even though some of these experiences and people seemed very real to me, I seriously question whether I was actually talking to people in heaven. I believe that these were prophetic experiences meant to convey a message. I do not know if the places I saw in heaven were actual places or appeared to me in the way that they did for the purpose of conveying that message. However, I am open to the thought that I saw real places and met real people. I see no conflict with Scripture that would prohibit this possibility, although I understand how some would object. Even so, just as Abel still speaks though he is dead, certainly the lives of biblical characters are messages, and these experiences helped to illuminate this to me more than ever before.

One reason that I lean toward the belief that these were prophetic experiences and that I was not talking with the real people is because of how long they did or did not last. For example, most people have had dreams that were so real that when they awoke, for a brief time they may actually believe that the dreams were real. However, even the most realistic of dreams usually begins to fade so that in just a couple of hours, it can be forgotten. Real experiences are not that way. I have had real encounters with the Lord and with angels that are almost as real to me now as they were years ago when I first experienced them. I have had many dreams and visions in which I saw the Lord or angels, but these would quickly fade. Except for a very few of my experiences included in these books, these prophetic episodes faded like revelations rather than enduring like real encounters.

It was for this reason that I tried to write down these experiences as quickly as I could after having them. In some cases, I was not able to do this. When I was able to get to a place where I could write them down, my memory of them had already begun to fade. I did feel the Holy Spirit helping to bring things to my remembrance, but the more time that elapsed between the experience and the time in which I was able to record them, the more concerned I was that they may have not been conveyed exactly as I received them.

In such cases, I was aware that my own pet doctrines or prejudices could easily creep into my writing, and though I sincerely tried not to let this happen, I acknowledge the possibility that this could have occurred in some instances. For this reason, my continual prayer for this book has been for the Holy Spirit to lead me in writing it and also to lead everyone who reads it. He was given to lead us to the truth and to Jesus. My prayer is that you will discern that which is truth and that which is from Jesus, holding fast to that which is and discarding anything that isn't.

## Infallibility of Scripture

Though there are many places where I tried to write the exact words of the Lord as they were spoken to me, this is not Scripture, and I do not believe that any prophetic experience is intended to carry the weight of Scripture. Even so, prophecy is very important for the church or we would not have been exhorted by the Scripture to **"Pursue love, yet desire earnestly spiritual gifts, but especially that you may *prophesy*" (I Corinthians 14:1).** We are told that **"But one who prophesies speaks to men for edification and exhortation and consolation. One who speaks in a tongue edifies himself; but one who prophesies edifies the church" (I Corinthians 14:3-4).** Never are we told that prophecy is for the purpose of teaching doctrine—we have the Scriptures for that. Never are we told that prophecy is infallible, which is why we must judge prophecy. However, prophecy does edify.

Because prophecy is a gift of the Holy Spirit, we must treat everything that comes from Him as holy, but because it comes through humans, it must not be considered infallible.

The Scriptures, as they were originally written, are infallible. They are the rock of truth and pure revelation of God and His ways upon which we can build our lives with the surety that Scripture will stand forever. I view prophecy more like the manna that the Lord served in the wilderness. It is from the Lord and will help to sustain us in our day-by-day walks, but if we try to keep it longer than intended, it will become foul.

The Scriptures are permanent and given so that we can build our lives upon truth, while prophecy is given for edification and encouragement, strategically keeping us in the day-to-day will of the Lord. The quality of any relationship will be determined by the quality of the communication, and any relationship that does not have continuing communication is a dying relationship. Prophecy does help to keep our day-to-day relationship with the Lord fresh, which is why I believe that the Scripture encourages us to **"especially"** seek this gift.

I have sought the gift of prophecy for many years. I did this out of obedience to the Scripture that exhorts us to do this because I love the prophetic gifts. I love prophetic experiences, even though all but a few have been major rebukes for me. Even so, I have prayed much more often for wisdom and the gift of a word of wisdom than I have for any of the other gifts. That is why I think that the Lord almost always appears to me in these experiences personified as Wisdom. I also think that a truly wise person loves rebukes, because **"reproofs for discipline are the way of life" (Proverbs 6:23)**. In every one of these experiences, I received a profound and badly needed correction in my life.

In this book, there are also some very basic corrections for the church in general. Except for the churches for which I have personal responsibility, I try not to see the problems that are afflicting the body of Christ. The church is the Lord's bride, and I am very cautious about any way that I would presume to bring correction to her. Just as Paul explained to the Corinthians, we have spheres of authority within which we must stay.

It is not right for me to correct someone else's children, but as a friend, I may speak to the parents and hope that they also would feel the liberty to speak to me if they see things which need correcting in my children. However, in the experiences included in this book, the Lord showed me that the church today is headed for some terrible catastrophes if we do not make some very basic course corrections. I consider myself as having these problems, too, and therefore if you ask me what we should do about them, all I can say now is that I also am trying to work them out. I am seeking more revelation, a greater understanding in the interpretation, and the wisdom to apply all this correctly.

I encourage you again to keep in mind that even though the prophetic experiences I had when I received these messages were very real when they took place, they would often seem unreal to me only hours later. That was sometimes a problem when I tried to record these experiences. I did my best to write them as faithfully as I could, but I by no means claim that these are the exact words spoken to me or that everything written about these experiences is written exactly as they occurred. However, even though I may have forgotten some of the details or did not always get the wording right, the message is true, it is from the Lord, and the time is near.

**Rick Joyner**
**November 1998**

# CHAPTER I

# the glory

I stood looking at the door that I was to enter next. It was plain and uninviting. As I turned to view once again the Great Hall of Judgement, I was overwhelmed by its glory and expanse. I did not want to leave here even though the evil of my own heart was continually exposed. Although the process was painful, it was so liberating that I did not want it to stop. I actually yearned for more conviction.

*"And you shall have more,"* Wisdom interjected, knowing my thoughts. *"What you have found here will go with you. However, you do not have to come here to be changed. The power of the cross is enough to change you. What you have experienced here you can experience every day. The Holy Spirit was sent to convict you of sin, to lead you to truth, and to testify of Me. He is with you continually. You must get to know the Holy Spirit better.*

*"Many believe in the Holy Spirit, but few make room for Him in their lives. As the end of this age approaches that will change.*

*The Holy Spirit is about to move over the earth as He did in the beginning. He will take the chaos and confusion that are spreading across the earth, and He will bring forth the glorious new creation right in the midst of it. You are about to enter the times when He will do wonders continually, and the whole world will be in awe of His works.*

*"He will do all of this through My people. When the Holy Spirit moves, the sons and daughters of God will prophesy. From the old to the young they will dream dreams and see visions. The works that I did, and greater works, will they do in My name, that I might be glorified in the earth. The whole creation groans and travails for what the Holy Spirit is about to do.*

*"What you will find through that door will help you to prepare for what is to come. I am the Savior, but I am also the Judge. I am about to reveal Myself to the world as the Righteous Judge. First, I must reveal My judgment to My own household. My people are about to know the fellowship of the Holy Spirit. Then they will know His power to convict of sin. They will also know that He will always lead them to the truth that will set them free. This is the truth that testifies of Me. When My people have come to know Me as I AM, then I will use them to testify of Me.*

*"I am the Judge, but it is better for you to judge yourself so that I will not have to judge you. Even so, My judgments are about to be restored to My people. I will judge My own household first. After that I will judge the whole earth."*

The glory of Wisdom was overshadowing everything around me. I had never seen such splendor before, even here. It increased as He talked about His judgments. I knew by this that there was a glory to be seen by knowing Him as the Judge that was greater than I had known before. I started feeling so small and insignificant in His presence that it was hard for me to concentrate on what He was saying. Just when I thought I would be overwhelmed by His glory, He reached out and touched me on the forehead, gently but firmly. When He did this, my mind became focused and clear.

*"You began to look at yourself. This will always bring confusion, making it harder for you to hear Me. Every time you experience My touch, your mind will become clearer. Every time you feel My presence, know that I have come to touch you in order that you may see Me and hear Me. You must learn to abide in My presence without becoming self-conscious and self-absorbed. This causes you to turn from the truth that is in Me and turn to the deception that is in your fallen nature.*

*"Many people fall when My Spirit touches them. The time for falling is over. You must learn to stand when My Spirit moves. If you do not stand when My Spirit moves, He cannot use you. The heathen should fall before Me, but I need for My people to stand so that I can use them."*

## The Pride of False Humility

I heard irritation in the Lord's voice when He said this. I felt that it was like the irritation He seemed to have with His disciples in the gospels. Immediately I understood that His irritation usually came when they started looking at their inadequacies or failures.

"Lord, I'm sorry," I pleaded, "but your presence is so overwhelming. How do I keep from feeling so small when I'm close to you like this?"

*"You are small, but you must learn to abide in My presence without looking at yourself. You will not be able to hear from Me or speak for Me if you are looking at yourself. You will always be inadequate. You will always be unworthy for what I call you to do, but it will never be your adequacy or worthiness that causes Me to use you. You must not look at your inadequacy, but look to My adequacy. You must stop looking at your own unworthiness and look to My righteousness. When you are used, it is because of who I am, not who you are.*

*"You did feel My anger as you began to look at yourself. This is the anger I felt toward Moses when he started to complain about how inadequate he was. This only reveals that you are looking to yourself more than to Me, which is the main reason why I am able to use so few of My people for what I desire to do. This false humility is actually a form of the pride that caused the fall of man. Adam and Eve began to feel inadequate and that they needed to be more*

32

*than I had made them to be. They took it upon themselves to make themselves into who they should be. You can never make yourself into who you should be, but you must trust Me to make you into who you should be."*

Although I had never related false humility to the fall of man in the Garden, I knew that this was a major stumbling block preventing many from becoming useful to the Lord, and I had taught on this many times. Now in His presence, my own false humility was revealed in me and looked even worse than I had ever seen it in anyone else. This form of pride was repulsive, and I could understand why it caused the anger of the Lord to burn.

In His presence, all that we are is soon revealed, and even after all of the judgment I had just endured, I still had some of the most basic flaws that kept me from knowing Him and serving Him as I was called to do. As shocking as this was, I did not want to dwell on myself any longer, so I turned to look at Him, desiring to see as much of His glory as I could endure while He was with me in this way. Immediately, my gloom turned into ecstasy. My knees wanted to buckle, but I was determined to stand for as long as I could.

Soon after, I awoke. For days afterward, I felt an energy surging through me making everything look glorious. I loved everything that I saw. A doorknob seemed wonderful beyond comprehension. Old houses and cars were so beautiful to me that I was sorry I was not an artist so that I could capture their beauty and nobility. Trees and animals all seemed like very special personal friends. Every person I saw was like a library of revelation and meaning, and I was so thankful for eternity so that I could get to know them all. I could not look at anything without seeing magnificence, hardly believing that I had walked through so much of my life and missed so much.

Yet, for all of this wonderful emotion and revelation I felt flowing through me, I did not know what to do with it. I knew that if I did not learn how to use it for good that it would fade, which it did in just a few days. It was as if the meaning of life was slipping from me, and I knew that I had to recover it. What I had experienced was more wonderful than any drug, and I was addicted. This was the result of seeing His glory, and I had to see more. I desired to learn how to *abide* in His presence and to allow His life to flow through me in order to touch others. I had to abide in the Holy Spirit and allow Him to use me. *This was my call.*

# CHAPTER II

# two
# witnesses

For days I had been in a deep depression. Everything seemed so bleak. Even the very sound of people irritated me, and any disruption to what I wanted to do angered me. I thought the worst of everyone and had to fight to contain the black thoughts that arose in me toward them. I felt as if I had slipped into hell and was sliding deeper into it each day. I finally cried out to the Lord and almost immediately found myself standing in front of the door with Wisdom standing next to me.

"Lord, I am sorry. I slipped from Your presence all the way into hell it seems."

*"The whole world still lies in the power of the evil one,"* He replied, *"and you walk on the edge of hell every day. Through the midst of it, there is a path of life. There are deep ditches on either side of the path of life, so you must not deviate from the narrow way."*

"Well, I fell into one of the ditches and could not find my way out."

*"No one can find their own way out of those ditches. Following your own way is how you fall into them, and your own way will never lead you out. I am the only way out. When you fall, do not waste your time trying to figure everything out, for you will only sink deeper into the mire. Just ask for help. I am your Shepherd, and I will always help you when you call on Me."*

"Lord, I don't want to waste time trying to figure everything out, but I would really like to understand how I fell so far, so fast. What caused me to turn from the path of life and fall into the ditch like that? You are Wisdom, and I know that it is wisdom to ask."

*"It is wisdom to know when to ask for understanding and when to just ask for help. Here it is wisdom for you to ask. Only when you are in My presence can you understand. Your understanding will always be twisted when you are depressed, and you will never accurately see truth from that place. Depression is the deception that comes from seeing the world from your perspective. Truth comes from seeing the world through My eyes from where I sit, at the right hand of the Father. Like the cherubim in Isaiah 6, those who abide in My presence will say, 'The whole earth is filled with His glory.'"*

I remembered how as a new believer, I had read this text and actually thought that these cherubim were deceived. I could not understand how they could say *"The whole earth is filled with His glory,"* when the whole earth seemed to be filled with wars, disease, child abuse, treachery and evil on every side. Then the Lord spoke to me one day and said, *"The reason that these cherubim say that the whole earth is filled with My glory is because they dwell in My presence. When you dwell in My presence, you will not see anything but glory."*

"Lord, I remember you teaching me that, but I have not lived it very well. I have spent much of my life seeing things from the dark side. I guess I have spent much of my life sitting in one of those ditches beside the path of life rather than walking on it."

*"That is true,"* the Lord responded. *"Every now and then you would get up and take a few paces, but then slide off into the ditch on the other side. Even so, you have made some progress, but now it is time for you to stay on the path. You do not have any more time to waste in those ditches."*

The Lord's kindness and patience seemed overwhelming as He continued.

*"What caused you to slide into the ditch this last time?"* He began.

After thinking about it, I could see that I had become consumed with maintaining the feeling rather than knowing the Source of the feeling.

"I took My eyes off of you," I confessed.

39

*"I know it seems too simple, but this is all that you did, and taking your eyes off of Me is all that you have to do to drift from the path of life. When you abide in Me, you will see nothing but glory. This does not mean that you will not see the conflicts, confusion, darkness and deception that are in the world, but when you see them, you will always see My answer to them. When you abide in Me, you will always see how truth prevails over deception, and you will see the manner in which My kingdom will come."*

"Lord, when I am here, this is all more real to me than anything I have experienced on earth, but when I am on earth, all that is here seems like an unreal dream. I know that this is the true reality and that earth is temporary. I also know that if this place were more real to me on earth, I would be able to walk in your wisdom more and stay on the path of life. You have said it is always wisdom to ask. I ask you to make this realm more real to me when I am on the earth. Then I will be able to walk more perfectly in your ways. I also ask you to help me to convey this reality to others. The darkness is growing great on earth, and there are few who have vision. I ask You to give us more of Your power, let us see more of Your glory, and let us know the true judgment that comes from Your presence."

*"When you start to live by what you see with the eyes of your heart, you will walk with Me, and you will see My glory. The eyes of your heart are your window into this realm of the Spirit. Through*

*the eyes of your heart, you may come to My Throne of Grace, at any time. If you will come to Me, I will be more real to you. I will also trust you with more power."*

As He spoke, I was compelled to turn and look at the multitudes of kings, princes, friends and servants of the Lord who were all standing in the Hall of Judgment. The wonder and glory of all that occurred there were so great that I would have been satisfied to stay forever. Again I was astounded to think that this place was just the beginning of heaven. But even with all of its wonders, the real wonder of heaven was the presence of the Lord. Here in the beginning of heaven, He was Wisdom and He was the Judge, which are the same.

"Lord," I inquired, "Here you are Wisdom and the Judge, but how are you known in the other realms of heaven?"

*"I AM Wisdom and I AM the Judge in every realm, but I AM also much more. Because you have asked, I will show you who I AM. Even so, you have only begun to know Me as Wisdom and Judge. In due time, you will see more of Me, but there is more for you to learn about My judgments first."*

## The First Witness

"God's judgments are the first step into the heavenly realm," a voice said that I had not heard before. "When the Judgment Day comes, the King will be known to all, and His judgments will be understood. Then the earth will be set free.

You asked for His judgments to come to your own life, now begin asking for them to come to the world."

I turned to see who had spoken. He was of great stature and brilliance, but a little less than the others I had met in the Hall of Judgment. I assumed that he was an angel, but then he said:

"I am Lot. You have been chosen to live in difficult times just as I was chosen. As Abraham lived and interceded for Sodom, you must do the same. During the times when great perversion is released upon the earth, men and women of great faith will also arise. Like Abraham, you must use your faith to intercede for the wicked, and you must also witness the judgment of God coming upon the earth. The Lord cannot abide the increasing evil of mankind much longer. I was silent and many perished. You must not be like me—you must not be silent."

"Tell me more. How do I warn them?" I asked.

"I thought that I would be a warning just by being different. Being different is not enough! The power of the Holy Spirit to convict of sin is released by the spoken word. What the Lord did to Sodom, He did as an example so that others would not have to be destroyed in this way. You can warn those who are headed for destruction by telling them my story. There are now many cities whose evil He will not abide much longer. If those who know the Lord do not arise, there will be many more like Sodom very soon.

"The Judgment Day is coming. All of creation will then know the wisdom of His judgments, but you must not wait for that day. You must seek His judgments every day, and you must make them known on the earth. If His people will walk in His judgments, many on the earth will know of them before the great Day of Judgment. By this many more will be saved. It is His desire that none should be lost, and that none of His people suffer loss on that day.

"The people of the earth are blind. They will not see if you simply try to be a witness. The message of judgment must go forth in *words*. The Holy Spirit anoints words, but the words must be spoken in order for Him to anoint them. "Righteousness and justice are the foundation of His throne. His people have come to know something of His righteousness, but few know His justice. His throne will abide in His house, therefore judgment must begin with His own house.

"You must live by the truth that you have learned here, and you must teach it. His judgments are coming. If His people will walk in His judgment before the Judgment Day, that day will be glorious for them. If they do not live by them, they, too, will know the sorrow that the world is about to know. His judgments would not be true if they were not the same for all. Through you and others, He will entreat His people again to judge themselves lest they be judged. Then you must entreat the world."

Lot directed me to look at the door before which I was standing. It still seemed dark and uninviting, like the doctrines of God's judgment, I thought. The glory of the Lord that surrounded us made it seem even more bleak. Even so, I now knew how glorious His judgment really is. I had also come to understand that almost every door through which He leads us looks bleak at first and then becomes glorious. It almost seems that the bleaker the door looks, the more glorious it will be on the other side. Just passing through His doors takes faith, but they always lead to more glory.

Lot continued with my train of thought. As I had already learned, in this place thoughts are broadcast to all.

"Through that door, you will experience more of His glory. His glory is not just the brilliance that you see around Him or in this place, nor is it merely the feelings that you have while abiding in Him. His glory is also revealed through His judgments. This is not the only way that it is revealed, but it is this way that you were called here to understand. Through that door, you will learn of another way to see His glory. It is by seeing His glory that His people will be changed, and He is about to show them His glory. When they see His glory, they will rejoice in all of His ways, even in His judgments."

## The Second Witness

Then a second voice spoke, "I, too, confirm this truth. The judgment of God is about to be revealed on the earth. Even so, 'Mercy triumphs over judgment.' The Lord always extends mercy before judgment. If you will warn the people that His judgments are near, His mercy will save many."

I did not recognize the one speaking, but it was another man of great stature and nobility, with a brilliance that indicated a high rank.

"I am Jonah," he said. "When you understand the Lord's judgments, you understand His ways. However, even if you understand them, it does not mean that you agree with them. Understanding is necessary, but it is not enough. The Lord also wants you to agree with Him.

"You have often asked for the Lord's presence to go with you. That is wisdom. I was a prophet, and I knew Him, yet I tried to flee from His presence. That was a great folly, but not as foolish as you may think. I had come to understand the great burning that comes with His presence. I had come to understand the responsibility that comes from being close to Him. In His presence, all wood, hay and stubble is consumed. When you draw close to Him with hidden sin in your heart, it will drive you to insanity, as many have learned through the ages. I was not trying to flee from the will of the Lord as much as I was fleeing from His presence.

"When you ask for the reality of His presence, you are asking for the reality that you have seen here to be with you. Heaven is your true home, and it is right for you to yearn for this. Even so, He is a holy God, and if you will walk closely with Him, you, too, must be holy. The closer that you get to Him, the more deadly hidden sin can be."

"I understand this," I replied. "That is why I asked for the Lord's judgments in my own life."

"Now I must ask you this," Jonah continued. "Will you seek Him? Will you come to Him?"

"Of course," I responded. "I desire His presence more than anything. There is nothing greater than being in His presence. I know that many of my motives for wanting to be with Him are selfish, but being with Him helps to set me free from that kind of selfishness. I do want to be with Him. I will come to Him."

"Will you?" Jonah continued. "Until now you have been even more foolish than I was. You can come boldly before His Throne of Grace at any time and for any need, but rarely do you come. Yearning for His presence is not enough. You must come to Him. If you draw near to Him, He will draw near to you. Why do you not do it? You are always as close to Him as *you* want to be.

"Many have come to know and follow His ways, but they do not come to Him. In the times that you will soon enter, they will depart from His ways because they did not come to Him. You have laughed at my folly, which was great, but yours is even greater than mine. However, I do not laugh at your folly—I weep for you. Your Savior weeps for you; He intercedes for you continually. When He weeps, all of heaven weeps. I weep because I know how foolish His people are. I know you because you are just like me, and like me, the church has run to Tarshish, desiring to trade with the world even more than sitting before His glorious throne. At the same time, the sword of God's judgments are hanging over the earth. I weep for the church because I know you so well."

"I am guilty!" I pleaded. "What can we do?"

"Great storms are coming upon the earth," Jonah continued. "I slept when the storm came upon the ship that I was in while running from the Lord. The church is also sleeping. I was the prophet of God, but the heathen had to wake me up. So it is with the church. The heathen have more discernment than the church at this time. They know when the church is going the wrong way, and they are shaking the church, trying to wake you up so that you will call on your God.

"Soon the leaders of the world will cast you overboard, just as the men in that ship had to do to me. They will not let you keep going in the way you are headed. This is the grace of God to you. He will then discipline you with a great beast that comes up out of the sea. It will swallow you for a time, but you will be vomited out of it. Then you will preach His message."

"Is there no other way?" I asked.

"Yes, there is another way," Jonah replied, "although this has come and is coming. Some are already in the belly of the beast. Some are about to be cast overboard, and some are still sleeping, but almost all have been on the ship going the wrong way, seeking to trade with the world. However, you can judge yourself and He will not have to judge you. If you will wake yourself up, repent and go the way that He sends you, you will not have to be swallowed by the beast."

"Is the beast to which you are referring the one in Revelation 13?" I asked.

"It is the same. As you read in that chapter, this beast is given to make war with the saints and to overcome them. This will happen to all who do not repent. But know that those who are overcome by this first beast will be vomited out of it before the next beast comes, the one that comes up out of the earth. Even so, it will be much easier for you if you repent. It is much better not to be swallowed by the beast.

"Just as Lot's story is a warning to those who are given over to perversion, my story is a warning to the Lord's prophet, the church. The church is running from the presence of the Lord. It is running to activity in place of seeking the Lord's presence. You may call your activity 'ministry,' but it is actually running from the presence of the Lord. As I have said, the church is running to Tarshish so that it can trade with the world and seek the treasures of the sea, while the greater treasures—the treasures of heaven—few are seeking.

"The sin of wanting to trade with the world has entangled the church, just as I was entangled in the belly of the beast with the weeds wrapped around my head. The weeds, the cares of the world, have wrapped themselves around the mind of the church. It took me three days to turn to the Lord because I was so entangled. It is taking Christians much longer. Their minds are so entangled with the world, and they have fallen to such depths, that many have no hope of getting free. You must turn to the Lord instead of away from Him. He can untangle *any* mess, and He can bring you up from the greatest depths. Run *from* Him no longer! Run *to* Him!"

Then Lot added, "Remember the mercy that the Lord had for Nineveh. He had mercy because Jonah preached. He did not live among them and try to be a witness: He preached the Word of God. Power is in the Word. There is no darkness so dark that His Word cannot penetrate it. Many will repent and be saved if you will go to those to whom the Lord sends you and give His warning."

Then Jonah continued, "When you fall short of the Lord's grace and sin entangles you, it is hard for you to come to Him. You must learn to always run to the Lord at such times, not away from Him. When you go through that door, you will enter the times when the Lord's power and glory will be released on the earth such as He has not done since the beginning of time. All of heaven has been waiting for the things that you are about to see. It will also be the time of the greatest darkness. You cannot endure either the glory or the darkness without His grace. You will not walk in His ways without coming to Him daily. You must not only seek His presence, but you must abide in His presence continually.

"Those who have tried to follow Him by just seeking Him once a week in a church service while they spend the rest of the week seeking the world will soon fall away. Those who call upon His name thinking that He is their servant also will soon fall away. He is the Lord of all and all will soon know this! First, His own people must know it, so the judgment is going to begin with His own household.

"It is presumption to only call upon the Lord when you want something. You should call on Him to ask what He wants, not what you want. Many of those who have some faith also have great presumption; the line between the two can be very thin. When God's judgments come to His own household, His people will learn the difference between faith and presumption. Those who try to do His work without Him will fall away. Many have faith in the Lord, but only know

Him from a distance. These do great works in His name, but He does not know them. Those who have known Him from afar will soon weep over their folly.

"God does not exist for the sake of His house—His house exists for Him. In His patience, He has been waiting outside of His own house, knocking, calling, but few have opened to Him. Those who hear the Lord's voice and open to Him will sit with Him at His table. They will also sit with Him on His throne, and they will see the world as He sees it. Presumption cannot sit with Him at His table, nor on His throne. Presumption is the pride that caused the first fall, and all of the darkness and evil that are about to be reaped on the earth have come because of it.

"When Satan saw God's glory, he turned to the way of presumption. Satan dwelt in His presence and still turned from Him. This is the greatest danger for those who see His glory and know His presence. Do not become presumptuous because of what you have seen. Never become proud because of your visions: This will always lead to a fall."

## Merciful Judgment

As Jonah spoke, each word was like a hammer blow. I was appalled by my sin. Not only was I ashamed of the way in which I had thought of him, but I was ashamed even more for mocking Jonah for the very same things that I, too, had done.

51

Even though I tried desperately to stand, my knees could not hold me up any longer, and I fell to my face. His words were like being flailed with a whip, but at the same time, the pain was welcome. I knew I needed to hear them, and I did not want Jonah to stop teaching me until all of my evil ways were exposed. The exposing power of the words was great, but it was much more than that. There was a power on them that made any excuse seem appalling. They passed every barrier and went straight to my heart. As I lay on the ground, I felt as though I were undergoing surgery.

Then Lot interjected, "Many believers have made falling down in the Lord's presence frivolous and meaningless, but the church is about to fall under the same power that felled you—conviction. If you fall when you cannot stand then your falling will result in your standing for truth."

Still I did not want to move. I did not want to do anything until I had firmly grasped what Jonah had said. I did not want the conviction to go away until it had done its work. They seemed to understand as there was silence for a time, and then Lot continued.

"Jonah had the greatest preaching anointing yet given to a man. Without miracles or signs, when he preached, one of the most wicked cities that ever existed repented. If Jonah had preached in Sodom, that city would have remained until this day. The power of Jonah's preaching is a sign. When he awakened and was vomited out of the beast, he had this power. This is the power of preaching that will be given to the church in the last days. This is the power of conviction that the Lord is waiting to give His church. When she is vomited out of the beast that has swallowed her, even the most evil will listen to her words. This is the sign of Jonah that will be given to the church. The words of those who experience resurrection from the deep will have power." *I have given thee Power; says the Lord*

I was still stunned. Even so, I was determined to run to the Lord and not away from Him, so I turned to look directly at Wisdom.

"Lord, I, too, can fall away in what is coming! I am guilty of all of these things. I have seen so much of your glory, and still I fall to the traps and diversions that keep me from drawing close to you. Please help me in this. I desperately need Your wisdom, but I also need Your mercy. Please send mercy and help us before You send the judgment that we deserve. I ask for the mercy of the cross."

Wisdom answered, *"You will be given mercy because you have asked for it. I will give you more time. My mercy to you is time. Use this time wisely, for soon there will be no more. The time is near when I can delay no longer. Every day that I delay My judgment is mercy. See it as that and use it wisely.*

*"I would always rather show mercy than judgment, but the end is near. The darkness is growing and the time of great trouble will*

*be upon you soon. If you do not use the time I give you, the coming troubles will overtake you. If you use the time that I give you wisely, you will overcome and prevail. There is one characteristic that is common to the overcomers in every age—they did not waste their time!*

*"In My mercy, I am giving you this warning. Warn My people that in My mercy, I will no longer let them presume on My mercy. In My mercy, My discipline will be upon them. Warn them not to harden their hearts, but to repent and turn to Me.*

*"It is true that you, too, can fall away. Your love will grow cold and you will deny Me, if you do not deny yourself and take up your cross every day. Those who seek to save their own life will lose it, but those who lose their life for My sake will find true life. What I will give to My people will be a life of even more abundance than they have asked for, even in their presumption.*

*"When I have finished judging My own household, I will then send My judgments upon the whole earth. In My righteous judgment, I will show a distinction between My people and those who do not know Me. Now the whole world lies in the power of the evil one. Now he rewards unrighteousness and resists the righteous. When the Judgment Day comes, the whole world will know that I reward righteousness and resist the proud.*

*"Righteousness and justice are the foundation of My throne. It is because of My justice that I discipline more severely those who know the truth but do not live by it. I have brought you here to see*

*My judgments. You have gained understanding here, but this will be an even greater judgment to you if you do not walk in what you have seen. To whom much is given, much will be required. Here you have known the mercy of My judgments. If you continue to allow sin to entangle you, you will know the severity of My judgment. Many of My people still love sin. Those who love sin and their own comfort and prosperity more than Me will soon know My severity. These will not stand in the times that are coming.*

*"I will show severity to the proud and mercy to the humble. The greatest distraction of My people has not been the difficulties, but the prosperity. If My people would seek Me during times of prosperity, I could trust them with even more of the true wealth of My kingdom. I desire for you to have an abundance for every good deed. I want your generosity to overflow. My people will prosper in earthly riches in the times ahead, even in the times of trouble, but the riches will be from Me and not the prince of this present evil age. If I cannot trust you with earthly riches, how can I trust you with the powers of the age to come? You must learn to seek Me as much in prosperity as when you are in poverty. All that I entrust to you is still Mine. I will only entrust more to those who are more obedient.*

*"Know that the prince of darkness also gives prosperity. He continues to make the same offer to My people that he made to Me. He will give the kingdoms of this world to those who will bow down and worship him and serve him by living according to his ways. There is a prosperity of the world and there is the prosperity of My*

*kingdom. The coming judgments will help My people to know the difference. The riches of those who have prospered by serving the prince of this evil age and using the ways of this evil age will be a millstone that hangs about their neck when the floods come. All will soon be judged by the truth. Those who prosper by Me do not compromise truth in order to prosper.*

*"My judgment begins with My household to teach you discipline so that you will walk in obedience. The wages of sin is death, and the wages of righteousness are peace, joy, glory and honor. All are about to receive their worthy wages. This is the judgment, and it is justice that it begins with My own household."*

Then Lot and Jonah spoke together, "'Behold now the kindness and the severity of God.' If you are going to know Him more, you are going to know both of these more."

Conviction was coming upon me like a cascade, but it was a cascade of living water. It was cleansing and refreshing, and it was difficult. I also knew that His correction would preserve me through what I was about to encounter after entering through the door. I desperately wanted all of the correction I could get before I entered it. I knew that I would need His correction, and I was right.

# CHAPTER III

# the path of life

I was pondering the things that had been spoken by Lot and Jonah when the Lord began to speak.

*"You asked to know the reality of this place even as you walk in the earthly realm. This is the reality for which you asked—to see as I see. It is not this place that is the reality. Reality is wherever I am. My presence gives any place true reality and made everything you looked at seem so alive because I am Life. My Father made Me the Life of all creation, both in the heavens and on the earth. All of creation exists through Me and for Me, and apart from Me, there is no life, and there is no truth.*

*"I am the Life that is in creation. I am even the Life in My enemies. I AM. All that exists does so through Me. I AM the Alpha and the Omega; I AM the Beginning and I AM the End of all things. There is no truth or reality apart from Me. It is not just the reality of this place that you seek, but the reality of My presence. You seek the true knowledge of Me, and this knowledge gives life.*

59

*This reality is just as available to you in the earthly realm as it is here, but you must learn not to just look for Me, but at Me.*

*"I am the power of God. I am the revelation of His glory. I am life and I am love. I am also a person. I love My people and want to be with them. The Father loves Me and He also loves you. He loves you so much that He gave Me for your salvation. We want to be close to you. We love mankind and Our eternal dwelling place will be with you. Wisdom is knowing Me, knowing the Father, and knowing Our love. The light, the glory and the power that I am about to reveal in the earth will be released through those who have come to know My love.*

*"My Father has entrusted Me with all power. I can command the heavens and they obey Me, but I cannot command love. Love commanded is not love at all. There will be a time when I demand obedience from the nations, but then the time to prove your love will have passed. While I am not demanding obedience, those who come to Me obey Me because they love Me and love the truth. These are the ones who will be worthy to reign with Me in My kingdom, those who love Me and serve Me in spite of persecution and rejection. You must want to come to Me. Those who become Our dwelling place will not come because of a command, or just because they know My power—they will come because they love Me and they love the Father.*

*"Those who come to the truth will come because they love Us and want to be with Us. It is because of the darkness that this is the*

*age of true love. True love shines the brightest against the greatest darkness. You love Me more when you see Me with your heart and obey Me, even though your eyes cannot see Me as they do now. Love and worship will be greatest in the great darkness that is coming upon the earth. Then all of creation will know that your love for Me is true and why we desire to dwell with men.*

*"Those who come to Me now, fighting through all the forces of the world that rebel against Me, come because they have the true love of God. They want to be with Me so much that even when it all seems unreal, even when I seem like a vague dream to them, they will risk all for the hope that the dream is real. That is love. That is the love of the truth. That is the faith that pleases My Father. All will bow the knee when they see My power and glory, but those who bow the knee now when they can only see Me dimly through the eyes of faith are the obedient ones who love Me in Spirit and in truth. These I will soon entrust with the power and glory of the age to come, which is stronger than any darkness.*

*"As the days grow darker upon the earth, I will show more of My glory. You will need this for what is coming. Even so, remember that those who serve Me even when they do not see My glory are the faithful, obedient ones to whom I will entrust My power. Obedience in the fear of God is the beginning of wisdom, but the fulness of wisdom is to obey because of your love for God. Then you will see the power and the glory.*

*The entire, whole, and full reason that Rick recieved this was because of Jesus' Prophet.*

*Jer 23:28 The*

"You are not here because of your faithfulness. Even the humility that caused you to pray for My judgments was a gift. You are here because you are a messenger (prophet). Because I have called you for this purpose, I gave you the wisdom to ask to know My judgments. It is wisdom for you to be faithful to what you see here, but the greatest wisdom is for you to come to Me every day. The more you come to Me, the more real I will be to you. I can be as real to you on the earth as I am to you now, and when you know the reality of My presence, you are walking in truth.

## I AM

"Now you see Me as the Lord of Judgment. You must also see Me as the Lord of the Sabbath. I AM both. You must know Me as the Lord of Hosts and behold My armies, and you must see Me as the Prince of Peace. I AM the Lion of Judah, and I AM also the Lamb. To know My wisdom is also to know My times. You are not walking in wisdom if you are proclaiming Me to be the Lion when I want to come as the Lamb. You must know how to follow Me as the Lord of Hosts into battle, and you must know when to sit with Me as the Lord of the Sabbath. To do this, you must know My times, and you can only know My times by staying close to Me.

"The coming judgment for those who call upon My name but do not seek Me will be that they will increasingly fall out of timing with Me. They will be at the wrong place, doing the wrong things, and even preaching the wrong message. They will try to reap when

*it is time to sow and sow when it is time to reap. Because of this, they will bear no fruit.*

*"My name is not I WAS, nor is it I WILL BE, but I AM. To really know Me, you must know Me in the present. You cannot know Me as I AM unless you come to Me every day. You cannot know Me as I AM unless you abide in Me.*

*"Here you have had a taste of My judgments. You are about to see Me in other ways. You will not be able to fully know Me as I AM until you live in eternity. Here the different aspects of My nature all fit together perfectly, but they are hard to see when you are in the realm of time. This Great Hall reflects a part of Me that the world is about to see. This will be an important part of your message, but it will never be all of it. In one city, I will send My judgment, but in the next I may send mercy. I will send famine to one nation and abundance to another. To know what I am doing, you must not judge by appearances, but from the reality of My presence.*

*"In the times that are now coming upon the earth, if your love for Me is not growing stronger, it will grow cold. I AM life. If you do not stay close to Me, you will lose the life that is in you. I AM the Light. If you do not stay close to Me, your heart will grow dark.*

*"All of these things you have known in your mind, and you have taught them. Now you must know them in your heart, and you must live them. The springs of life issue from the heart, not the mind. My wisdom is not just in your mind, nor just in your heart. My*

*wisdom is the perfect union of both mind and heart. Because man was made in My image, his mind and heart can never agree apart from Me. When your mind and heart agree, I will be able to trust you with My authority. Then you will ask what you will and I will do it because you will be in union with Me.*

*"Because of the difficulty of the times in which you are called to walk, I have given you the experience of beholding My Judgment Seat before the appointed time of your judgment. Now your prayer has been answered. What you did not understand was that during the time when you were waiting for Me to answer this prayer, I was answering it every day through all that I allowed to happen in your life.*

*"It is better to learn of My ways and My judgments through the experiences of life than to learn of them in this way. I have given you this experience because you are a messenger and the time is short. You already knew what you have learned here, but you did not live by that knowledge. I have given you this experience as mercy, but you must choose to live by it.*

*"I will use many messengers to teach My people to live in righteous judgment so that they do not perish when My judgments come upon the earth. You must hear My messengers and obey their words that are from Me without delay, for the time is now short. To hear them without obeying will only bring a more severe judgment upon you. This is righteous judgment. To whom much is given, much will be required.*

*"These are the times when knowledge increases. Knowledge of My ways is also increasing with My people. Your generation has been given more understanding than any other generation, but few are living by their understanding. The time has come when I will no longer tolerate those who say they believe Me, but do not obey Me. The lukewarm are about to be removed from among My people. Those who do not obey Me do not really believe in Me. By their lives, they teach My people that disobedience is acceptable.*

*"As Solomon wrote, 'Because the sentence against an evil deed is not executed quickly, therefore the hearts of the sons of men among them are given fully to do evil.' This has happened to many of My own people, and their love has been growing cold. My judgments are going to come more swiftly as grace to keep My people's hearts from giving themselves fully to evil. They are about to know that the wages of sin is death. They cannot continue to call on Me to deliver them from their troubles when they still love sin. I will give a little more time to judge yourself so that I will not have to judge you, but that time is short.*

*"Because you have been here, even more will be required of you. I will also impart more grace to you to live by the truth that you know, but you must come to My Throne of Grace every day to get it. I say to you again, the time has come upon the earth when no one will be able to stand in truth without coming to My Throne of Grace each day. What I am about to tell you is so that you and those who are with you cannot only live, but stand and prevail. As My people*

*stand and prevail over the time of darkness that is coming, the creation will know that light is greater than darkness.*

*"Life and death have been planted in the earth, and life and death are about to be reaped. I came to give you life. The evil one comes to give death. In the times ahead, both will be seen in their fulness. I will therefore give those who obey Me an abundance of life such as has never been seen on earth before. There will be a distinction between My people and those who serve the evil one. Choose life that you may live. Choose life by obeying Me. If you are choosing Me and the light that is in you is My true light, it will grow brighter every day. By this you will know that you are walking in My light. The seed that is planted in good soil always grows and multiplies: You will be known by your fruit."*

# CHAPTER IV

# truth and life

As the Lord spoke, His glory seemed to increase. It was so great that at times, I thought I was going to be consumed by it. His glory burned, but it was not like a fire; it burned from the inside out. I somehow knew that I would either be consumed by His glory or by the evil I would face after I went through the door. His words were penetrating and gripping, but I knew that it was even more important to behold His glory, so I was determined to do just that for as long as I could.

He appeared more brilliant than the sun. I could not see all of His features because of the brightness, but as I continued to look, my eyes adjusted some to His brilliance. His eyes were like fire, but not red; they were blue, like the hottest part of the fire. They were fierce, yet had the attraction of an endless wonder.

His hair was black and sparkled with what I thought at first were stars, and then I realized that it glistened with oil.

I knew that this was the oil of unity, which I had seen in a vision before. This oil radiates like precious stones, but is more beautiful and more valuable than any earthly treasure. As I looked at His face, I felt the oil begin to cover me, and as it did, the pain of the fire of His glory was more bearable. It seemed to impart peace and rest, and only came upon me as I looked at His face. When I looked away from His face, it would stop.

I felt compelled to look at His feet. They also were like flames of fire, but were more of a bronze or golden flame. They were beautiful, but also fearsome, as if they were about to walk with the most fearful of strides. As I looked at His feet, I felt like an earthquake was going off inside of me, and I knew that as He walked, everything that could be shaken would be shaken. I could only stand it for a moment, and then I had to fall on my face.

When I looked up, I was looking at the door. Now it was even less attractive than before. At the same time, I felt a desperation to go through it before I would choose not to. It was my calling to go through the door, and to not go would be to not obey. In His presence, even the *thought* of disobedience seemed to be such a base selfishness more repulsive than the thought of returning to the battle of the earthly realm.

As I looked at the door, I heard another voice begin to speak which I did not recognize. I turned to see who was speaking. He was one of the most naturally attractive people I had seen yet, regal and strong.

"I am Abel," he said. "The authority that the Lord is about to give His people is the anointing for true unity. When there were just two brothers on the earth, we could not live in peace with one another. From my time until yours, mankind has walked in the way of increasing darkness. Murder will be released on the earth as never before. Even your World Wars were but birth pangs leading to what is to come. But remember this: Love is stronger than death. The love that the Father is about to give to those who serve Him will overcome death."

"Please, tell me everything that you have been given to tell me," I responded, knowing that he had much to say.

"My blood still speaks. The blood of every martyr still speaks. Your message will live on if you trust in the life that you have in God more than you trust in the life that you have on earth. Do not fear death, and you will overcome it. Those who do not fear death will have the greatest message during the times you are entering when death is released on the earth.

I thought of all of the wars, famines and plagues that had come upon the earth just in my century. "How much more can death be released?" I asked.

Abel continued without answering me, which I understood to be the answer. "The blood sacrifice has already been made for you. Trust the power of the cross, for it is greater than life. When you trust the cross, you cannot die. Those on earth have power for a time to take your earthly life, but they cannot take your life if you have embraced the cross.

"A great unity will come to the Lord's people who dwell on the earth. This will take place when His judgments come upon the earth. Those who are in unity will not only endure His judgments, but they will prosper because of them. By this He will use His people to warn the earth. After the warnings, He will then use His people as a sign. Because of the discord and conflict that arise in the darkness, the unity of His people will be a sign that the whole earth will see. His disciples will be known by their love, and love does not fear. Only true love can bring true unity. Those who love will never fall. True love does not grow cold, but true love does grow."

**Love Releases Life**

Another man who looked almost exactly like Abel came and stood beside him.

"I am Adam," he said. "I was given authority over the earth, but I gave it to the evil one by obeying evil. He now rules in my place and your place. The earth was given to man, but the evil one has taken it. The authority I lost was restored by the cross. Jesus Christ is 'the last Adam,' and He will soon take His authority and rule. He will rule through mankind because He gave the earth to mankind. Those who live in your times will prepare the earth for Him to rule."

"Please tell me more," I asked, a little surprised to see Adam, but wanting to hear everything he had to say. "How do we prepare for Him?"

"Love," he said. "You must love one another. You must love the earth, and you must love life. My sin released the death that now flows as rivers upon the earth. Your love will release rivers of life. When evil reigns, death is stronger than life, and death prevails over life. When righteousness reigns, life prevails, and life is stronger than death. Soon the life of the Son of God will swallow up the death that was released through my disobedience. It is not just living that you must love, but *life*. Death is your enemy. You are called to be a messenger of life.

"When the Lord's people begin to love, He will use them to release His judgments. His judgments are to be desired. The whole world is groaning and travailing as it waits for His judgments, and when they come, the world will learn righteousness. What He is about to do, He will do through His people, and His people will stand as Elijah in the last days. Their words will shut up the heavens or bring rain; they will prophesy earthquakes and famines, and they will come to pass; they will stop famines and earthquakes.

"When they release armies in the heavens, armies will march on the earth. When they hold back armies, there will be peace. They will decide where He shows mercy and where He shows His wrath. They will have this authority because they will love, and those who love will be one with Him. What you will see through that door is to help prepare you for what He is about to do through His people.

"I know authority. I also know the responsibility of authority. Because of the great authority that I was given, I am responsible for what has happened to the earth. Even so, the grace of God began to cover me, and God's great redemption will soon swallow up my mistake. Peace will be taken from the earth, but you are called to help restore it. Peace prevails in heaven, and you are called to bring heaven to earth. Those who abide in His presence will know peace and will spread peace.

"The earth itself will shake and tremble. Times of trouble greater than have ever been known will begin to move across the earth like great waves of the sea. Even so, those who know Him will not be troubled. They will stand before the raging of the seas and say, 'Peace, be still' and the seas will be calm. Even the least of His little ones will be like a great fortress of peace that will stand through all that is coming. His glory will be revealed to His people first and then through them. Even the creation will recognize Him in His people and will obey them as it does Him.

"This is the authority that I had, and it will be given to mankind again. I used my authority to turn Paradise into a wilderness. The Lord will use His authority to turn the wilderness into Paradise again. This is the authority that He is giving to His people. I used mine wrongly and death came. When His authority is used in righteousness, it will release life. Be careful how you use authority. With authority comes responsibility. You, too, can use it wrongly, but you will not do this if you love. As all of heaven knows, 'Love never fails.'"

"What about the earthquakes, famines and even wars that you said we would release on the earth? Won't this be releasing death?" I asked.

"All the death that is coming upon the world is being allowed to prepare the way for life. Everything that is sown must be reaped, unless those who have sown evil call upon the cross in Spirit and truth. The army of the cross is about to be released, and it will march in the power of the cross, carrying the offer of mercy to all. Those who reject the mercy of God have rejected life."

"That is a great responsibility," I said. "How do we know when they have rejected His mercy?"

"Disobedience brought death, and obedience will bring life. When I walked with God, He taught me His ways. As I walked with Him, I began to know Him. You must walk with God and learn of His ways. Your authority is His authority, and you must be one with Him in order to use it. The weapons of His army are not carnal—they are spiritual and much more powerful than any earthly weapons. Your most powerful weapons are truth and love. Even the final judgment of destruction is God's love extended in mercy.

"When truth spoken in love is rejected, death has been chosen over life. You will understand this as you walk with Him. You will come to understand the Spirit that He has given to you to bring life and not death. There is a time to give men over to reap what they have sown, but you must do all things in obedience. Jesus came to give *life*. He does not desire for any to perish, and this must be your desire also. For this reason, you must even love your enemies if you are to be trusted with the authority that He wants to give to His people.

"The time is at hand for the fulfillment of what has been written. His people have prayed for more time, and He gave it to them. However, few have used it wisely. You have a little more time, but soon the time can no longer be delayed. The time is near when time itself will seem to speed up. As it is written, when He comes, He will come quickly. However, you are not to fear the times. If you fear Him, you do not need to fear anything that is coming upon the earth.

"All that is about to happen is coming so that His wisdom can again prevail on earth just as it does in heaven. All of the evil that was sown in mankind is about to be reaped. Even so, the good that He has sown will also be reaped. Goodness is stronger than evil. Love is stronger than death. He walked the earth to destroy the works of the devil, and He will finish what He has begun."

## Power and Love

As Adam talked, I was captured by his grace and dignity. I began to wonder if he had possibly lived his whole life after the fall without sinning again because he seemed to be so pure. Knowing my thoughts, he changed the subject briefly to answer them.

"I lived long on the earth because sin did not have a deep root in me. Even though I had sinned, I was created to walk with God, and my desire was still for Him. I did not know the depths of sin that the following generations knew. As sin grew, life was shortened, but in every generation, those who walk with God touch the life that is in God. Because Moses walked so closely with God, he would have lived on had the Lord not taken him. Enoch walked with Him so closely that the Lord had to take him as well. That is why Jesus said, 'I am the resurrection and the life; he who believes in Me shall live even if he dies, and everyone who lives and believes in Me shall never die.'

"What you are seeing in me is not just the lack of sin, but the presence of life that I had on the earth. What we were on earth will remain a part of who we are forever. I can look at all of the others here who are a part of the great cloud of witnesses and know much about their life on earth."

"So you are a part of the great cloud of witnesses."

"Yes. My story is a part of the eternal gospel. My wife and I were the first to taste sin, and the first to see our children reap the consequences of disobedience. We have beheld the death spread through each generation, but we have also beheld the cross and seen the victory over sin.

"Satan has boasted since the cross that Jesus could *redeem* men but could not *change* them. During the times of the greatest darkness and evil that are about to come, His people will stand as a testimony for all time that He not only redeemed His people from sin, but He also removed sin from them. Through them, He will remove sin from the whole earth. He will now display to the whole creation the power of His new creation. He did not come just to forgive sin, but to save mankind from sin, and He is returning for a people who are without stain from the world. This will come to pass in the most difficult of times.

"I was created to love the Lord and to love the earth, as were all people. I have loathed the sight of the world's rivers becoming sewers. Even more have I loathed the sight of what has happened to the human mind. The philosophies of the human mind now filling the streams of human thought are as loathsome as the sewage filling the rivers. But the rivers of human thought will one day be pure again, just as the rivers of the earth. By this, for all time to come, it will be proven that good is stronger than evil.

"The Lord did not go to the cross just to redeem, but also to restore. He walked the earth as a man to show mankind how to live. He will now reveal Himself through His chosen ones to show them who they were created to be. This demonstration will not just come through power, but through love. He will give you power because He is all powerful, and power is also a revelation of Him. Even so, He uses His power because of love and so must you. Even His judgments come because of love. When you send them forth, it must be because of love. Even His final judgment of the earth will be His final mercy."

I looked at Adam, Abel, Lot and Jonah as they stood together. I knew that it would take forever to understand the depths of the revelation of the great gospel of God that each of their lives represented. Adam's disobedience made the way for Abel's obedience, whose blood still speaks as a harbinger

79

of salvation. Righteous Lot could not save a city, while an unrighteous Jonah could. Like the four gospels, there seemed to be no end to the understanding that could be learned from them. This, too, was my call.

# CHAPTER V

# the DOOR

*"I love this book", I said.*

*"Yes, it is My Bright and Morning Star, My Word, thus saith God (a revelation of Jesus the Word)*
*1/27/03*
*4:19 p.m.*

I tried desperately to absorb every word these men had spoken to me. Never had Wisdom said so much to me at once, yet I felt that every sentence was crucial, and I did not want to forget anything. I thought about how good it would be to have His words carved in stone like Moses and to carry the words of the Lord to His people in such a way that they could be preserved untainted by me. Again knowing my thoughts, Wisdom answered them.

*"That is the difference between the Old Covenant and the New. You will write My words in a book and they will inspire My people. Even so, the true power of My words can only be seen when they are written in the hearts of My people. Living epistles are more powerful than letters written on paper or stone. Because you are not writing Scripture, the words you write will have you in them. Even so, your books will be as I desire them to be because I prepared you for this task. They will not be perfect because perfection will not*

*come to the earth until I come. For perfection, men will have to look to me. Even so, My people are the book that I am writing, and the wise can see Me in My people, and in their works.*

*"My Father sent Me into the world because He loves the world, and I am sending My people into the world because I love the world. I could have judged the world after My resurrection, but the course of the world was allowed to continue so that My righteous ones could be proven and the power of what I did on the cross would be seen in mankind. I did this because of love. You are the witnesses of My love. This is My commandment to you: Love Me and love your neighbor. Only then will your witness be true. Even when I command you to speak of My judgments, it must be in love.*

*"The life of every person is in My book, and their lives are a book that will be read by all of creation for all eternity. The history of the world is the library of God's Wisdom. My redemption is the demonstration of Our love, and the cross is the greatest love that the creation will ever know. Even the angels who stand before My Father so love the story of redemption that they, too, long to dwell with men. They marveled when We made man in our image. They marveled when men chose evil, even in the midst of the Paradise We had made for man. Now, because of redemption, the marred image of God is restored and is revealed even more gloriously in mankind. The glory is still in earthen vessels which makes the glory easier to see for those who have eyes to see.*

*"This is the new creation that is greater than the first creation. Through My new creation, we are making a new Paradise that is greater than the first Paradise. Every man, woman and child that embraces My redemption is a book that I am writing which will be read forever. Through the new creation, We will also restore the former creation, and it will be a paradise again. I will restore all things, and all evil will be overcome with good.*

*"My church is the book that I am writing, and the whole world is about to read it. Until now, the world has wanted to read the book that the evil one has written about My church, but soon I will release My book.*

*"I am about to release My last-day apostles. I will have many like Paul, John, Peter and the others. To prepare them, I am sending many like John the Baptist who will teach them devotion to Me and lay the foundation of repentance in their lives. These apostles will also be like John the Baptist. Just as the chief joy of John's life was to hear the voice of the Bridegroom, these will have one devotion— to see My bride made ready for Me. Because of this, I will use them to build highways through the wilderness and rivers through the deserts. They will bring down the high places and raise up the lowly. When you go through that door, you will meet them.*

*"I am about to release My last-day prophets. They will love Me and walk with Me, even as Enoch did. They will demonstrate My power and prove to the world that I am the One true God. Each will be a pure well from which only living waters flow. At times,*

*their water will be hot for cleansing; at times, it will be cold for refreshing. I will also give them lightening in one hand and thunder in the other. They will soar like eagles over the earth, but they will descend upon My people like doves because they will honor My family. They will come upon cities like whirlwinds and earthquakes, but they will give light to the meek and lowly. When you go through that door, you will also meet them.*

*"I am about to release My last-day evangelists. I will give them a cup of joy that will never run out. They will heal the sick and cast out devils; they will love Me and love righteousness; they will carry their crosses every day, not living for themselves but for Me. Through them, the world will know that I live and that I have been given all authority and power. These are the fearless ones who will attack the gates of the enemy and raid the dark places of the earth, leading many to My salvation. These, too, are just beyond that door, and you will meet them.*

*"I am about to release shepherds who will have My heart for the sheep. These will feed My sheep because they love Me. They will care for each of My little ones as if they were their own, and they will lay down their own lives for My sheep. This is the love that will touch men's hearts—when My people lay down their lives for one another. Then the world will know Me. I have given these choice food to serve My household. These are the faithful ones that I will trust to watch over My own house. These, too, are beyond that door, and you will meet them.*

*"I am about to release My last-day teachers upon the earth. They will know Me and teach My people to know Me. They will love the truth. They will not retreat before the darkness, but they will expose it and drive it back. They will unstop the wells that your fathers dug, and serve the pure waters of life. They will also carry out the treasures of Egypt and use it to build My dwelling place. You will meet these, too, just beyond that door."*

As the Lord spoke, I looked at the door. Now, for the first time, I wanted to go through it. Each word that He spoke brought a rising expectation in my heart, and I badly wanted to meet these last-day ministers.

*"You have known in your heart for many years that these are coming. I have brought you here to show you how to recognize them and help them on their way."*

I went through the door.

# CHAPTER VI

# the prison

Suddenly, I was standing in a large prison yard. There were huge walls such as I had never seen before. They extended for as far as I could see, hundreds of feet high and very thick. There were other fences and razor wire in front of the wall. Every few hundred feet there were guard towers along the top of the wall. I could see guards in each one, but they were too far away for me to see much about them.

It was grey, dark and dreary, which seemed to perfectly reflect the mass of people who stood in the prison yard. All over the yard, people sat in groups of their own kind. Old black men were in one group, young black men in another. Old and young white men also stayed apart, and the women were also separated. With every race, this seemed to be the same. Those with any distinguishing characteristic were separated, except for the youngest children.

Between the groups, many people seemed to be milling around. As I watched, I could tell that they were trying to find their own identity by finding the group which they were the most like. However, it was obvious that these groups did not let anyone join them easily.

As I looked more closely at these people, I could see that they all had deep wounds and many scars from previous wounds. Except for the children, they all seemed to be nearly blind and could only see well enough to stay in their own group. Even within their groups, they were constantly trying to see the differences that others might have. When they found even a small difference, they would attack the one who was different. They all seemed hungry, thirsty and sick.

I approached an older man and asked him why they were all in prison. He looked at me in astonishment, declaring emphatically that they were not in prison, and why would I ask such a stupid thing. I pointed at the fences and the guards, and he replied, "What fences? What guards?" He looked at me as if I had insulted him terribly, and I knew that if I asked him anything else, I would be attacked.

I asked a young woman the same question and received the same response. I then realized that they were so blind that they could not even see the fences or the guards. These people did not know that they were in prison.

## The Guard

I decided to ask a guard why these people were in prison. As I walked toward the fences, I could see holes in them that would be easy to climb through. When I reached the wall itself, I found it so irregularly built that it was easy for me to climb. Anyone could easily escape, but no one was trying because they did not know that they were captives.

When I got to the top of the wall, I could see for a great distance and saw the sun shining beyond the walls. It did not shine in the prison yard because of the height of the wall and the clouds that hung over it. I saw fires far off in the prison yard toward the end where the children were gathered. The smoke from these fires formed a thick cloud over the yard that turned what would have been just shade from the walls into a choking, dreary haze. I wondered what was burning.

I walked along the top of the wall until I reached the guard post. I was surprised to find the guard dressed in a fine suit with a collar indicating that he was some kind of minister or priest. He was not shocked to see me, and I think he assumed that I was another guard.

"Sir, why are these people in prison?" I asked.

That question shocked him, and I watched fear and suspicion come over him like a blanket.

"What prison?" he replied. "What are you talking about?"

"I am talking about those people in this prison yard," I said, feeling a strange boldness. "You're obviously a prison guard because you're in a guard house, but why are you dressed like that?" I continued.

"I am not a prison guard! I am a minister of the gospel. I am not their guard—I am their spiritual leader. This is not a guard house—it is the Lord's house! Son, if you think your questions are funny, I am not laughing!" He grabbed his gun and seemed ready to shoot at me.

"Please excuse me for disturbing you," I replied, sensing that he would definitely use his gun.

As I walked away, I expected to hear shots at any moment. The man was so insecure I knew he would shoot before thinking if he felt threatened. I could also tell that he was sincere. He really did not know that he was a guard.

## The School Teacher

I walked along the wall until I felt I was a safe distance away and turned to look back at the minister. He was pacing back and forth in his guardhouse, greatly agitated. I wondered why my questions disturbed him so much. It was obvious that my questions did not open him to seeing anything differently, but rather made him even more insecure and more deadly.

As I walked, I felt a desperation to find out what was going on and I thought about how I could rephrase my questions so as not to offend the next guard I tried to talk to. As I approached the next guard house, I was again surprised by the appearance of the guard. It was not another minister, but a young lady who was about 25 years old.

"Miss, may I ask you some questions?" I inquired.

"Certainly. What can I help you with?" she said with a condescending air. "Are you the parent of one of these children?"

"No," I responded. "I am a writer," which I somehow knew was the answer I should give her. As I expected, this got her attention.

Not wanting to make the same mistake I had made with the minister by calling what he was standing in a "guard house," I asked the young lady why she was standing in "that place." Her response was immediate, and she seemed surprised that I did not know.

"I'm a school teacher, so don't you think it quite natural that I should be in my school?"

"So this is your *school*," I replied, indicating the guard house.

"Yes. I've been here for three years now. I may be here the rest of my life. I love what I'm doing so much." This last remark was so mechanical that I knew I would discover something if I pressed her.

"What do you teach? It must be interesting for you to consider spending the rest of your life doing it."

"I teach general science and social studies. It is my job to shape the philosophy and world view of these young minds. What I teach them will steer them for the rest of their lives. What do you write?" she inquired.

"Books," I responded, "I write leadership books," anticipating her next question. I also somehow knew that if I had said, "*Christian* leadership books," our conversation would have ended. She seemed even more interested after this answer.

"Leadership is an important subject," she stated, still with a slightly condescending air. "Changes are happening so quickly that we must have the right leadership tools to steer these changes in the right direction."

"What direction is that?" I asked.

"Toward the prosperity that can only come through peace and security," she replied, as if she were surprised that I would even ask such a question.

"I don't mean to offend you," I replied, "but I'm interested in your views on this. What do you feel is the best way for this peace and security to be achieved?"

"Through education of course. We are together on this spaceship earth and we have to get along. Through education, we are helping deliver the masses from their caveman, tribal mentality to understand that we are all the same and that if we all do our part for society, we will all prosper together."

"That's interesting," I replied, "but we are not all the same. It is also interesting that all of the people down there are becoming even more divided and separated than ever. Do you think that it may be time to possibly modify your philosophy a bit?"

She looked at me in both amazement and agitation, but obviously not because she even considered for a moment that what I said was true.

"Sir, are you completely blind?" she finally responded.

"No, I believe I see quite well," I answered. "I have just come from walking among the people and have never seen such division and animosity between different people groups. It seems to me that the conflict between them is worse than ever."

I could tell that my statements were like slaps in the face to this young lady. It was as if she just could not believe someone was even saying these things, much less believing that there was a chance there might be some truth to them. As I watched her, I could tell that she was so blind that she could barely see me. She was in such a high tower that there was no way that she could see the people below. She really did not know what was going on, but sincerely thought that she could see everything.

"We are changing the world," she said with obvious disdain. "We are changing people. If there are still people acting like beasts such as you described, we will change them, too. We will prevail. Mankind will prevail."

"That is quite a responsibility for someone so young," I remarked.

She bristled even more at that statement, but before she could respond, two women appeared walking toward the door of the guard house along the top of the wall. One was a black woman who appeared to be in her fifties and the other was a very well-dressed white woman who was probably in her early thirties. They talked with each other as they walked, and both appeared confident and dignified. I could tell that they could see, which is obviously how they reached the top of the wall.

To my surprise, the young school teacher grabbed her gun and stepped outside of the guardhouse to meet them, obviously not wanting these women to get any closer. She greeted them with a very superficial cheerfulness and an obvious air of superiority that she seemed to want to impress on them. To my surprise, the two women became timid and overly respectful of one who was so much younger.

"We've come to ask about something our children are being taught that we do not understand," the black woman stated, mustering some courage.

"Oh, I'm sure that a lot is now taught that you do not understand," the teacher replied condescendingly.

The women kept looking at the teacher's gun which she handled in such a way so that they would constantly be aware of it. I was standing close by, amazed by this whole scene. The teacher turned and looked at me nervously. I could tell that she was afraid I might say something to the women. As she fingered the gun, she demanded that I leave. The women looked up to see to whom she was talking, and I realized that they could not see me. Their fear had blinded them.

I called out to the women, entreating them to have courage and believe what they felt in their heart. They looked in my direction as if they could only hear noise. They were losing their ability to hear as well. Seeing this, the young teacher smiled. She then aimed her gun at me and blew a whistle. I felt as if she perceived me to be the most dangerous person alive.

I knew that I could not wait for whoever she had called with her whistle. I also realized that if I just stepped back a little, I would be safe because this young teacher was so blind. I was right. I walked away with her screaming, blowing her whistle, and finally becoming so enraged that she began to shoot at the two women.

As I stood on top of the wall between two guard posts wondering about all of this, I felt the presence of Wisdom.

*"You must return to the prison yard. I will be with you. Know that you have the vision to escape any trap or weapon. Only*

*remember that fear can blind you. As you walk in the faith that I am with you, you will always see the way to go. You must also be careful to only reveal your vision to those to whom I lead you. Vision is what the guards fear the most. I know you want to ask me a lot of questions, but they will be better answered by the experiences you will have there."*

# CHAPTER VII

# the young apostle

I climbed down and began to walk through the yard. As I passed by the prisoners, they seemed almost completely disinterested in me or all of the commotion on the wall. I then remembered that they could not see that far. A young black man stepped into my path and looked at me with bright, inquisitive eyes.

"Who are you?" we both said at the same time.

As we stood looking at each other, he finally said, "My name is Stephen. I can see. What else do you want to know about me that you do not already know?"

"How could I know anything else about you?" I inquired.

"The one who helped me to see said that one day, others would come who were not prisoners. They would also be able to see, and they would tell us who we are and how we can escape from this prison."

I started to protest that I did not know who he was when I remembered what Wisdom had told me about those whom I would meet when I passed through the next door.

"I do know you, and I know some things about you," I acknowledged, "But I confess that this is the weirdest prison I have ever seen."

"But this is the only prison!" he protested.

"How do you know that if you have been here all of your life?" I asked.

"The one who helped me to see told me that it was the only one. He said that every soul who had ever been imprisoned was held captive here. He always told me the truth, so I believe this."

"Who is the one who helped you to see?" I asked, not only wanting to know who had helped him to see, but also interested in how this was the prison that held every soul captive.

"He never told me his real name, but just called Himself 'Wisdom.'"

"Wisdom! What did He look like?" I questioned.

"He was a young, black athlete. He could see better than anyone and seemed to know everyone here. It is strange, though. I have met others here who said that they have also met Wisdom, but they all described Him differently. Some said that He was white and others said that He was a woman. Unless there are many 'Wisdoms,' He is a master of disguise."

"Can you take me to Him?" I asked.

"I would, but I have not seen Him for a long time now. I am afraid that He has left or maybe even died. I have been very discouraged since He departed. My vision even started getting worse until I saw you. As soon as I saw you, I knew that everything He told me was true. He said that you knew Him, too, so why are you asking me so much about Him?"

"I do know Him! And be encouraged, your Friend is not dead. I will tell you His real name, too, but first I must ask you a few questions."

"I know that you can be trusted, and I know that you and others like you who are coming will want to meet everyone who can see. I can take you to some of them. I also know that you and the others are coming to help a lot of these other prisoners to see. I am surprised by one thing though."

"What is that?"

"You are white. I never thought that the ones who came to help us see and be set free would be white."

"I am sure that there are many others coming who are not white," I responded. "I can tell that you already have considerable vision, so I know you can understand what I am about to say."

## The Value of Vision

As I looked at Stephen to be sure he was listening, I was moved by how open and teachable he was, in striking contrast to the teacher who had been about his same age. This man will be a true teacher, I thought as I continued.

"When we get to the place of ultimate vision, we will not judge people by the color of their skin, gender or age. We will not judge others by appearances, but after the spirit."

"That sounds like what our teachers used to tell us," Stephen responded, a little surprised.

"There is a difference though," I continued. "They tried to make you think that we are all alike, but we were created different for a reason. True peace will only come when we respect the distinctions we have. When we really know who we are, we will never be threatened by those who are different. When we are free, we are free to show those who are different from us honor and respect, always seeking to learn from one another, just as you are now doing with me."

"I understand," Stephen replied. "I hope I didn't offend you by saying that I was surprised that you were white."

"No, I was not offended. I understand. I am encouraged that you were able to recognize me in spite of the color of my skin. But remember, every time we open our hearts to learn from those who are different, our vision will increase. Your eyes are already brighter than when we first met."

"I was just thinking about how quickly my vision is being restored," Stephen remarked.

"I now know why I am here." I added, "You must keep in mind that your vision is your most valuable possession. Every day you must do that which will help to increase your vision. Stay away from the people and things that make you lose your vision."

"Yes, like getting discouraged."

"Exactly! Discouragement is usually the beginning of the loss of vision," I said. "To accomplish our purposes, we must resist discouragement in any form. Discouragement blinds."

"When I began to see, I started to feel that I had a purpose, maybe even an important one," Stephen continued. "Can you help me to know what my purpose is?"

"Yes, I think I can. To know our purpose is one of the greatest ways that our vision grows. It is also one of our greatest defenses against things like discouragement which destroys vision. I think my main purpose here is to help you and the others whose vision is being restored to know their purpose. But first we need to talk about something even more important."

## Buried Treasure

When Stephen spoke, I could hear the voice of Wisdom, so I knew that this young man had been taught by the Lord. I also knew that he did not know the Lord's name and would have difficulty believing that Wisdom's name was Jesus. I knew that I would need wisdom just to share the name of Wisdom. I thought about the apostles, prophets, evangelists, pastors and teachers that Wisdom said I would meet when I went through the door. I never dreamed that I would meet them in a place like this. As I looked out over the great mass of people, I felt His presence. He was with me and even in the gloom of this terrible prison, excitement was welling up in me. This is what I have been prepared for, I thought.

"Stephen, what do you see when you look at this great mass of people?" I asked.

"I see confusion, despair, bitterness, hatred. I see darkness," he replied.

"That is certainly true, but look again with the eyes of your heart. Use your vision," I responded.

He looked for a long time and then said with some hesitation, "I now see a great field with buried treasure in it. The treasure is everywhere and in almost every form."

"That is right," I responded. "This is also a revelation of your purpose. You are a treasure hunter. Some of the greatest souls who ever lived are trapped here, and you will help find them and set them free."

"But how will I find them, and how will I set them free when I am not even free?"

"You already know how to find them, but it is true that you will not be able to set them free until you are free. That is your next lesson. You must also remember that you will always know your purpose in a situation by seeing with the eyes of your heart. What you see from your innermost being will always reveal your purpose."

"Is that how you knew I am to be a treasure hunter?"

"Yes. But you must be free before you can become who you were created to be. Why haven't you escaped through those holes in the fence?" I asked.

"When I first began to see, I saw the fences and the wall. I also saw the holes in the fences and have gone through them. When I got to the wall, I tried several times to climb it, but fear would overcome me because I am afraid of heights. I also thought that if I got over the wall, I would be shot."

"Those guards cannot see nearly as well as you think," I replied. "They are almost as blind as the people here."

This seemed to really surprise Stephen, but I could also tell that it opened his eyes even more.

"Can you see the top of the wall?" I asked.

"Yes, I can see it from here."

"I want you to remember this," I continued. "I have now been in many places. Call them different worlds, or realms, if you will. There is one important principle that I have found to be true in every place, and you must remember it for the rest of your life."

"What is it?"

"You can always go as far as you can see. If you can see the top of the wall, you can get there. When you get to the top of the wall, you will be able to see farther than you have ever seen before. You must keep going for as far as you can see. Never stop as long as you can still see farther."

"I understand," he replied immediately. "But I'm still afraid to climb that wall. It's so high! Is it safe?"

"I will not lie to you and tell you it is safe, but I know that it is much more dangerous *not* to climb it. If you do not use your vision by walking in what you see, you will lose it. Then you will perish here."

"How will I seek out the treasure that is here if I leave?"

"That is a good question, but it is also one which keeps many from fulfilling their purpose. I can only tell you now that you have a great journey you must complete first. At the end of your journey, you will find a door leading you back to this prison, just as I found. When you return, your vision will be so great that they will never be able to trap you here again. Your vision will also be great enough to see the treasure that is here."

# CHAPTER VIII

# the light

Stephen turned and looked again at the wall. "I still feel great fear," he lamented. "I don't know if I can do it."

"You have vision, but you lack faith. Vision and faith must work together," I said. "There is a reason why your faith is weak."

"Please tell me what it is! Is there something that will help my faith to grow as my vision increases?"

"Yes. Faith comes from knowing who Wisdom really is. You must know His true name. Just knowing His name will give you enough faith to get you over that wall to freedom. The better you get to know His name, the greater the obstacles and barriers you will be able to overcome on your journey. One day you will know His name well enough to move any mountain."

"What is His name?" Stephen almost begged.

"His name is Jesus."

Stephen looked at the ground, and then up in the air as disbelief seemed to come over him. I watched as the struggle went on between his heart and his mind. Finally he looked at me again, and to my great relief, he still had hope in his eyes. I knew that he had listened to his heart.

"I suspected it," he said. "In fact, the whole time you were talking, I somehow knew that you were going to say that. I also know that you are telling me the truth. But I have some questions. Can I ask them?"

"Of course."

"I have known many people who use the name of Jesus, but they are not free. In fact, they are some of the most bound people that I know here. Why?"

"That is a good question, and I can only tell you what I have learned on my own journey. I think that every case is different, but there are many who know His name, but do not know *Him*. Instead of drawing closer to Him and being changed by seeing Him as He is, they try to make Him into their image. Knowing the name of Jesus is much more than just knowing how to spell it or say it. It is knowing who He really is. This is where true faith comes from."

I could still see doubt in Stephen's eyes, but it was the good kind of doubt—the kind that wants to believe rather than the kind that wants to disbelieve. I continued.

"There are others who really love Jesus and start to sincerely get to know Him, but they also remain prisoners. These are the ones who let the wounds or mistakes suffered on the journey turn them back. These have tasted freedom, but they returned to prison because of disappointments or failures. You can easily recognize them because they are always talking about the past instead of the future. If they were still walking by their vision, they would not always be looking backward."

"I have met many of those," Stephen remarked.

"You need to understand something if you are ever going to have this question answered. If you are to fulfill your destiny, you cannot be overly discouraged or encouraged by others who use the name of Jesus. We are not called to place our faith in His people, but in Him. Even the greatest souls will disappoint us at times because they are still human.

"Many who are like those I just described can also become great souls. Vision and faith can be restored, even in those who have become the most discouraged and disappointed. As a treasure hunter, this is your job. We cannot discard any human being—they are all treasures to Him. However, to really know Him and walk in true faith, you must not judge Him by His people, either the best or the worst," I shared.

"I always thought of Jesus as the white man's God. He never seemed to do much for our people."

"He is not a white man's God—He was not even white Himself! But neither is He a black man's God. He created all and He is the Lord of all. When you start to see Him as the God of any one group, you have greatly reduced who He is, and you have greatly reduced your own vision."

## Faith and Obedience

I watched silently as Stephen wrestled with many other things in his heart. I continued to feel the presence of Wisdom, and I knew that He could explain all things much better than I could. Finally Stephen looked up at me, with the light shining brighter than ever in his eyes.

"I know that all of the questions that I have been wrestling with really do not have anything to do with who Jesus really is, but who people have said He is. I know what you are saying is true. I know that Jesus is the One who gave me vision and that He is Wisdom; I must find out for myself who He really is; I must seek Him; I must serve Him. I also know that He has sent you here to help me get started. What do I do?"

"Wisdom is here now," I began. "You heard Him when I spoke, just as I heard Him speaking through you. You already know His voice. He is your Teacher. He will speak to you through many different people, sometimes even through those who do not know Him. Be quick to hear and obey what He says. Faith and obedience are the same. You do not have true faith if you do not obey, and if you have true faith you will always obey.

"You said that you will serve Him. That means that you will no longer live for yourself, but for Him. In the presence of Wisdom, you know the difference between what is right and what is wrong. When you come to know Wisdom, you will also understand what is evil. You must renounce the evil that you have done in the past, as well as that which comes to tempt you in the future.

"You cannot live as others do. You are called to be a soldier of the cross. When you embraced His name and the truth of who He is; when that great light came into your eyes; when the peace and satisfaction began to flood your soul just a few moments ago, you were born again and began a new life. Wisdom has been speaking to you for sometime, guiding you and teaching you, but now He lives *in* you. He will never leave you again. But He is not your servant, you are His."

"I do feel Him!" Stephen acknowledged. "But how I would love to see Him again!"

"You can see Him with the eyes of your heart at any time. This is also your call—to see Him more clearly and to follow Him more closely. That is what the journey is for. On your journey, you will learn about His name, and the power of the cross. When you have been trained, you will return here in that power, and you will help to set many of these captives free."

"Will you still be here?"

"I do not know. Sometimes I will have work to do here, and sometimes I will have work to do helping others on their journeys. I might meet you again out there where you are going. I am also still on my own journey. This is part of it. On your journey, there will be many doors that you must go through. You never know where they will lead. Some may bring you back here. Some doors may take you into the wilderness which all must travel through. Some lead to glorious heavenly experiences, and it is tempting to always look for those doors, but they are not always the ones we need to help us fulfill our destiny. Do not choose doors by their appearance, but always ask Wisdom to help you."

Stephen turned his gaze upon the wall. I watched a smile appear.

"I can climb that wall now," he said. "I even look forward to the challenge. I must admit that I still feel the fear, but it does not matter. I know that I can climb it, and I cannot wait to see what is behind it. I know that I am free. I am no longer a prisoner!"

I walked with Stephen to the first fence. He was surprised to discover that there were not only holes in it, but that wherever he touched them, the fences would fall apart in his hand, making other holes.

"What are these fences made of?" he asked.

"Delusions," I explained. "Every time someone escapes through them, a hole is made for others to go through. You can go through the holes that are already here or make one yourself."

Stephen chose a place that was thick with barbed wire, stretched out his arms and walked straight into it, opening a large hole as he went. I knew that he would one day return here and lead many others out through the hole he was now making. Watching him was sheer joy. I felt the presence of Wisdom so strongly that I knew I would see Him if I turned around. I did, and I was right. The great joy I was experiencing could be seen on His face as well.

# CHAPTER IX

# freedom

As I stood next to Wisdom watching Stephen walk through the fences, he called out, "What is the wall made of?"

"Fear."

I watched Stephen stop and look at the wall. It was huge. Many never got past the fences, and I knew that this was a crucial test for Stephen.

Without looking back, he called out again, "Will you help me climb it?"

"I can't help you," I responded. "If I try to help you, it will only take you twice as long and be even harder. To conquer your fears, you must face them alone."

"The more I look up at it the worse it seems," I heard Stephen say to himself.

"Stephen, you have made your first mistake."

"What did I do?" he cried out dejectedly, already full of fear.

"You stopped."

"What do I do now? I feel like my feet are too heavy to move."

"Look at the hole you made in the fences," I said. "Now look at the top of that wall, and start walking. When you get to the wall, keep going. Do not stop to rest. There is no rest to be found by hanging on the side of that wall, so just keep climbing until you get to the top."

To my great relief, he started moving forward again. He was going much slower, but he was moving. When he got to the wall, he began to climb, slowly but steadily. When I knew that he was going to make it, I went to the wall and quickly climbed it so that I could meet him on the other side.

I knew Stephen would be thirsty, so I waited for him by a stream. When he got there, he was a little surprised to see me, but very glad. I was just as surprised to see the change in him. Not only were his eyes shining more brightly and clearly than ever, but he walked with a confidence and nobility that was stunning. I had seen him as a soldier of the cross, but I had not seen him as the great prince who he obviously was called to be.

"Tell me about it," I said.

"It was so hard to start walking again and then to keep walking, I knew that if I ever stopped, it might be too hard to ever start again. I thought about the ones you told me of, the ones who knew the name of the Lord, but had never climbed that wall to walk in faith in His name. I knew that I could become one of them. I decided that even if I fell, even if I died, I would rather die than stay in that prison. I would rather die than not see what is on this side and not make the journey that I am called to make. It was hard, even harder than I thought, but it is already worth it."

"Here, drink from this stream. You will find all of the water and food that you need on the journey. It will always be there when you really need it. Let the hunger and thirst keep you moving. When you find the refreshments, rest for as long as they last, and then keep going."

He drank quickly and then stood up, anxious to move on.

"I will not see you again for a time, so there are a few things that I must tell you now that will help you on the journey."

Stephen looked at me with a focus and brightness that was marvelous. Those who have known the greatest bondage will love liberty the most, I thought. I directed him to look at the highest mountain that we could see.

"You must now climb that mountain. When you get to the top, look for as far as you can see. Mark well what you see, and look for the path that will lead you to where you are going. Make a map of the way in your mind. That is where you are called to go."

"I understand," he replied. "But can it be seen from one of these lower mountains? I'm no longer afraid of climbing, but I am anxious to get on with the journey."

"You can see places from these lower mountains and get to those places much faster. You could choose to do that. It will take longer and be much harder to climb that high mountain, but from there you will be able to see much farther and see something much greater. The journey from the high mountain will also be more difficult and take longer. You are free, and you can choose either journey."

"You always take the highest mountain, don't you?" Stephen asked.

"I know now that it is always the best, but I cannot say that I have always chosen the highest mountain. I have often chosen the easiest, quickest way, and I was always sorry when I did. I now believe that it is wisdom to always choose the highest mountain to climb. I know that the greatest treasure is always at the end of the longest, most difficult journey. I think that you, too, are that kind of treasure hunter. You have overcome great fear. Now is the time to walk in great faith."

"I know that what you are saying is true, and I know in my heart that I must climb the highest mountain now or I will always choose that which is less than I could have had. I am just so anxious to get going and arrive at my destination."

"Faith and patience go together," I responded. "Impatience is really a lack of faith. Impatience will never lead you to the highest purposes of God. Good can be the greatest enemy of best. Now is the time to establish a pattern in your life of always choosing the highest and best. This is the way to remain close to Wisdom."

"What else are you supposed to tell me before I go?" Stephen asked, sitting on a rock, wisely choosing to be patient and receive all that he needed to know before he left. I thought that he might already know Wisdom better than I knew Him.

## A Warning

"There is another wisdom that is not the wisdom of God, and there is another one who calls himself 'Wisdom.' He is *not* Wisdom; he is our enemy. He can be difficult to recognize because he tries to appear as Wisdom, and he is very good at it. He comes as an angel of light, and he usually brings truth. He will have a form of truth, and he has wisdom, but it has taken me a long time to be able to distinguish them from *the* Truth and *the* Wisdom. I have learned that I can still be fooled by him if for one moment I start to think that I can't. Wisdom has told me that we can never outsmart the enemy—our defense is to learn to first recognize, and then resist him."

Stephen's eyes were wide as that "knowing" look came over him. "I know who you are talking about!" he interjected.

"I met a lot of people in the prison who followed that one. They were always talking about a higher wisdom, a higher knowledge. They always seemed like noble, fair people, but they felt foul. Whenever I told them about Wisdom, they said that they knew 'Wisdom,' too, and that he was their 'inner guide.' However, when I listened to them, I did not feel I was being led to freedom like they said, but rather to an even stronger bondage in that prison. I just felt darkness around them, not like the light I felt when I talked with Wisdom. I knew they were not the same."

"The true Wisdom is Jesus. You know that now. True wisdom is to seek Him. Any wisdom that does not lead you to Jesus is a false wisdom. Jesus will always set you free. The false 'Wisdom' will always lead you to bondage. However, true freedom often looks like bondage at first, and bondage usually looks like freedom at first."

"It's not going to be easy is it?" Stephen lamented.

"No. It is not going to be easy, and it is not supposed to be. Suspicion is not the same as true discernment, but if you are going to suspect anything, suspect what seems easy. I have not yet found 'easy' through any door or on any path that has been right. Taking the easy way may be the surest way to be misled. You have been called as a soldier, and you are going to have to fight. Right now the whole world is in the power of the false 'Wisdom,' and you will have to overcome the world to fulfill your destiny."

"Already I have had to do things that were harder than anything I have ever done before," Stephen reflected. "But you are right—it is hard, but it is worth it. I have never known such joy, such satisfaction, such hope. Freedom is hard. It is hard to have to choose which mountain I climb. Back there, I knew that I could have chosen to not climb that wall. I felt like the fear of making that choice was the wall inside of me. But once I had made the choice, I knew I would make it over the top. But does it ever become easier?"

"I don't think so, but somehow 'hard' gets to be more fulfilling. There can be no victory without a battle, and the greater the battle, the greater the victory. The more victories you experience, the more you start to look forward to the battles, and you rise even higher to face the bigger ones. What makes it easy is that the Lord always leads us to victory. If you stay close to Him, you will never fail. After every battle, every test, you are much closer to Him and know Him much better."

"Will I always feel that darkness when the false 'Wisdom' tries to mislead me?"

"I don't know. I do know that the darkness comes when he deceives us into self-seeking. When he deceived the first man and woman into eating from the Tree of the Knowledge of Good and Evil, the first thing they did was to look at themselves. Once the false 'Wisdom' can make us self-centered, our fall into bondage is sure. The deceiver always tries to get you to seek yourself. The call to fulfill our destiny is not for our sake, but for the Lord's sake and for the sake of His people."

"Has anyone ever made it to their destiny without being tricked?"

"I don't think so. Even the great Apostle Paul admitted to having been foiled by Satan. Peter was tricked a few times that were recorded in Scripture, and we do not know how many other times that were not recorded. But don't be overly concerned about being deceived. That is actually one of his biggest traps. He sidetracks many by having them fear more in his power to deceive than to have faith in the power of the Holy Spirit to lead them into all truth. Those who have fallen into this trap not only fall into increasing bondage to fear, but they will attack anyone who walks in the freedom that comes with faith. I am quite sure that you will not make it far up that mountain before they ambush you."

"And they know the name of Jesus?" Stephen asked, a little confused. "They must have known His name to get over that wall and to have gone that far. I mean, didn't they really know His name once?"

"I am sure they did. But stand and look throughout the valley ahead around every mountain. What do you see?"

"It looks like little prisons. It looks like there are many just like the one I came out of!"

"That's why I was surprised when you told me that Wisdom had said this was the only prison, but after I was there for just a little while I understood what He meant. Look at the high walls. Look at the fences. They are all the same. If you are captured along the way, they will not bring you back here. They know you would choose death over that, but they will take you to one of the other prisons. When you get close to them, it is hard to see that they are prisons from the outside, but inside they are all the same, with people divided and imprisoned by their fears."

"I'm glad you showed them to me," Stephen offered. "I did not even see the prisons when I was looking this way from the top of the wall or when I was looking for the mountain I am to climb. And you think I will be ambushed many times by those who will try to capture me and put me in one of them? And these people will be using the name of Jesus?"

"The Lord, Himself, warns in Scripture that in the last days many will come in His name, claiming that He is indeed the Christ, and yet they will deceive many. Believe me, there are many like that, and I do not believe that most of them know they are deceivers. I can tell you a characteristic I have seen in all those whom I have met—they quit while on their journey, stopping short of their destiny. It takes faith to keep going, and they chose to follow fear rather than faith. They begin to think that fear is faith and actually see the walls of fear around their prisons as strongholds of truth. Fear will do that to your vision and you can start to see strongholds that way. Few of these people are really dishonest. They are sincere, but they are deceived by one of the most powerful deceptions of all, *the fear of deception.*"

"Should I fight them?"

"I understand your question and have asked it many times myself. They destroy the faith of so many and do far more damage to the sojourners than all of the cults and sects combined. There will be a time when all such stumbling blocks will be removed, but for now they, too, are serving a purpose by making the way harder."

"Wisdom wants it to be harder? It is already so difficult just battling our own fears. Why does He want to make it harder by making us battle all of these fearful people as well?"

"The journey will be exactly as easy or hard as He wants it to be. This life is a temporary journey used to prepare those who will reign with Him over the age to come as sons and daughters of the Most High forever. Every trial is for the purpose of changing us into His image. One of the first things we must learn on this journey is not to waste a single trial, but to seize them as the opportunities that they are. If your path is more difficult, it is because of your high calling."

## The Necessity of Discipline

*"Many are called, but few are chosen. Many will come to the wedding feast, but few will be the bride."*

We turned to see Wisdom standing behind us. He appeared as the young athlete that Stephen had come to know.

*"Run the race that is set before you, and the prize will be greater than you can understand at this time. You know the discipline that it takes to prepare for the race. Now discipline yourself for righteousness. I have called all to run, but few run so as to win. Discipline yourself to win."*

Then He was gone.

"Why did He leave?" Stephen asked.

"He said all that needed to be said at this time. He spoke to you of discipline. I would take that to be a most important word for you at this time."

"Discipline. I used to hate that word!"

"He spoke to you about the race. Were you a runner?"

"Yes, I am very fast. I was always the fastest one in my school and was even offered a scholarship to run for a major university."

"I take it that you did not accept it."

"No, I didn't."

"Was it because of a lack of discipline that you did not go to college?"

"No! It was..." There was a long silence as Stephen looked down at his feet. "Yes, I think it probably was."

"Don't worry about that now. However, you must understand something. Most who are potentially the best in every field or occupation never even become high achievers for the lack of that one thing—discipline. What you are doing now is much more important than track or college. Obviously discipline has been a weakness of yours, and it has cost you much already, but in Christ all things become new. In Him, the very things that have been your greatest weaknesses can become your greatest strengths. You are now His disciple. That means that you are 'a disciplined one.'"

"I know that you are telling me the truth, and I know that this is one race I do not want to lose."

"Do you see the path leading up the mountain?"

"Yes."

"Its name is Discipline. Stay on it if you want to reach the top."

# CHAPTER X

# the army

Suddenly, I was standing on a high mountain overlooking a great plain. Before me, there was an army marching on a wide front. There were 12 divisions in the vanguard that stood out sharply from the great multitude of soldiers who followed behind them. These divisions were further divided into what I assumed to be regiments, battalions, companies and squads. The divisions were distinguished by their banners, and the regiments were distinguished by their different colored uniforms.

Battalions, companies and squads were distinguished by such things as sashes or epaulets that each different group wore. All wore armor that was polished silver, shields that appeared to be pure gold, and weapons that were both silver and gold. The banners were huge, 30 to 40 feet long. As the soldiers marched, their armor and weapons flashed in the sun like lightening, and the flapping of the banners and the tread of their feet sounded like rolling thunder. I did not think that the earth had ever witnessed anything like this before.

Then I was close enough to see their faces—male and female, old and young from every race. There was a fierce resolution on their faces, yet they did not seem tense. War was in the air, but in the ranks I could sense such a profound peace that I knew that not a single one feared the battle to which they were marching. The spiritual atmosphere that I felt when close to them was as awesome as their appearance.

I looked at their uniforms. The colors were brilliant. Every soldier also wore rank insignias and medals. The generals and other higher ranking officers marched in the ranks with the others. Although it was obvious that those with higher rank were in charge, no one seemed overly sensitive to their rank. From the highest ranking officer to the lowest, they all seemed to be close friends. It was an army of what seemed to be unprecedented discipline, yet it also seemed to be just one big family.

As I studied them, they seemed selfless—not because they lacked identity, but because they were all so sure of who they were and what they were doing. They were not consumed with themselves or seeking recognition. I could not detect ambition or pride anywhere in the ranks. It was stunning to see so many who were so unique, yet in such harmony and marching in perfect step. I was sure that there had never been an army on earth like this.

Then I was behind the front divisions looking at a much larger group that was composed of hundreds of divisions. Each of these was a different size, with the smallest numbering about two thousand and the largest in the hundreds of thousands. Although this group was not as sharp and colorful as the first one, this also was an awesome army simply because of its size. This group also had banners, but they were not nearly as large and impressive as those of the first group's. They all had uniforms and ranks, but I was surprised that many of these did not even have on a full set of armor, and many did not have weapons. The armor and weapons that they did have were not nearly as polished and bright as those of the first group.

As I looked more closely at those in these ranks, I could see that they were all determined and had purpose, but they did not have nearly the focus of the first group. These seemed much more aware of their own rank and the rank of those around them. I felt that this was a distraction hindering their focus. I could also sense ambition and jealousy in the ranks, which unquestionably was a further distraction. Even so, I felt that this second division still had a higher level of devotion and purpose than any army on earth. This, too, was a very powerful force.

Behind this second army, there was a third one which marched so far behind the first two armies that I was not sure they could even see the groups ahead of them. This group was many times larger than the first and second armies combined, seemingly composed of millions and millions. As I watched from a distance, this army would move in different directions like a great flock of birds, sweeping first one way and then the next, never moving in a straight direction for very long. Because of this erratic movement, it was drifting farther and farther from the first two groups.

As I came closer, I saw that these soldiers had on tattered, dull gray uniforms which were neither pressed nor clean. Almost everyone was bloody and wounded. A few were attempting to march, but most just walked in the general direction in which the others were headed. Fights were constantly breaking out in the ranks causing many of the wounds. Some of the soldiers were trying to stay close to the frayed banners scattered throughout their ranks. Even so, not even those near the banners had a clear identity because they were constantly drifting from one banner to another.

In this third army, I was surprised that there were only two ranks—generals and privates. Only a few had a piece of armor on, and I did not see any weapons except dummy weapons which were carried by the generals. The generals flaunted these dummy weapons as if having them made the officers special, but even those in the ranks could tell that the weapons were not real. This was sad because it was obvious that those in the ranks desperately wanted to find someone who was real whom they could follow.

There did not seem to be any ambition except among the generals. This was not because of selflessness as in the first army, but because there was so little caring. I thought that at least the ambition present in the second group would be much better than the confusion that prevailed in this group. The generals here seemed to be more intent on talking about themselves and fighting with one another, which the little groups around the banners were constantly doing. I could then see that the battles within the ranks were the cause of the great sweeping, erratic changes of directions that this group would make from time to time.

As I looked at the millions in the last group, I felt that even with their great numbers, they did not actually add strength to the army, but rather weakened it. In a real battle, they would be much more of a liability than an asset. Just sustaining them with food and protection would cost more in resources than any value they could add to the army's ability to fight. I thought that a private in the first or second group would be worth more than many generals from the third. I could not understand why the first groups even allowed

this group to tag along behind them. They obviously were
not true soldiers.

## The Wisdom of Zipporah

I was suddenly on a mountain where I could see the entire
army. As I watched, I noticed that the plain was dry and dusty
before the army, but immediately after the first twelve
divisions passed, the earth was dark green, with trees giving
shade and bearing fruit and pure streams flowing throughout
the land. This army was restoring the earth. I thought of how
different this was from what would happen when one of the
world's armies would pass through a land. They would
plunder and forage until the land was utterly stripped
wherever they had marched.

I watched as the second divisions passed over the same
ground. They left bridges and many buildings, but the
ground was not left in as good of shape as before they had
passed. The grass was not as green, the streams were
somewhat muddied, and much of the fruit had been taken.

Then I saw what happened as the third group passed over
the same ground. The grass was either gone or so trampled
into the earth that it could not be seen. The few trees that
remained were stripped. The streams were polluted. The
bridges were broken down and impassable. The buildings
were left in shambles. It seemed that this group had undone

all of the good that the first two had done. As I watched them, anger welled up inside of me.

I felt Wisdom standing beside me. He did not say anything for a long time, but I could sense that He also was angry.

*"Selfishness destroys,"* He finally said. *"I came to give life and to give it abundantly. Even when My army has matured, there will be many who call on My name and follow those who follow Me, but they do not know Me or walk in My ways. These destroy the fruit of those who follow Me. Because of this, the world does not know whether to consider My people a blessing or a curse."*

As Wisdom said this, I felt immense heat coming from Him, intensifying until it was so painful that it was hard for me to concentrate on what He was saying. Even so, I knew that I was feeling what He was feeling and that it was an important part of the message which He was conveying to me. The pain was a combination of compassion for the earth and anger at the selfishness in this army. Both feelings were so strong that I felt as though they were being branded into me.

As the anger of the Lord continued to rise, I felt that He might destroy the entire army. Then I remembered how the Lord had met Moses when he was on his way to Egypt in obedience to the Lord. The Lord sought to put him to death until his wife, Zipporah, circumcised their son. I had never understood this until now. Because circumcision speaks of the removal of the fleshly, or carnal nature, the incident with

Moses was like a prophetic foreshadowing of the sin of Eli, the priest, who had brought a curse upon himself and defeat to Israel because he had failed to discipline his sons.

"Lord, raise up those with the wisdom of Zipporah!" I cried out.

The burning continued and a deep determination came over me to go to the leaders of this great army and tell them the story of Zipporah and that everyone in the Lord's army had to be circumcised in their hearts. The carnal nature had to be cut away. I knew that if they marched any farther before this was done, the entire army was in danger of being destroyed by the Lord Himself, just as He had almost killed Moses when he was returning to Egypt.

Then I was standing in the Hall of Judgment before the Judgment Seat. The Lord still appeared as Wisdom, but I had never seen Him more fierce, nor His words come with more weight.

*"You have already seen this army in your heart many times. The leaders I am commissioning now will lead this army. I am sending you to many of these leaders. What will you say to them?"*

"Lord, this is a great army, but I am still grieved about the condition of the third group. I do not understand why they are even allowed to pretend to be a part of Your army. I would like to say that before they went any farther, the first and second armies should turn and drive away this third group. They were really very little more than a huge mob."

*"What you saw today is still in the future. The ministries I am about to release will gather this army and equip them to be all that you saw. At this time, almost My entire army is in the condition of the third group. How can I let them be driven away?"*

I was stunned by this, although I knew that I had never seen any of the Lord's people who were in as good shape as even the second group of this army.

"Lord, I know I felt Your anger at this group. If almost Your entire army is now in that condition, I am just thankful that You have not destroyed all of us. When I was looking at this third group, I felt that their deplorable condition was due to a lack of training, equipping and vision, as well as a failure to embrace the cross that circumcises the heart. I believe I must go to them with the message about Zipporah, but they also need drill sergeants and officers who will train them."

Wisdom continued, *"Remember the first army that you saw before the mountain. They, too, were unprepared for the battle, and when the battle began, those who were not prepared fled. However, many returned with their armor on and their delusions replaced with truth. The first two groups in this army were also changed by battles that woke them up to their true condition. Then they cried out to Me and I sent them shepherds after My own heart.*

*"All of My shepherds are like King David. They are not hirelings who seek their own place or position, but they will lay down their lives for My people. They are also fearless in warfare against My enemies and pure in their worship of Me. I am about to send these shepherds forth. You must return with the message of Zipporah. The time is coming soon when I will not abide those who seek to be counted with My people who do not circumcise their hearts. You must warn them of My wrath.*

*"I am also sending you back to walk with the prophets I am sending forth as Samuels to pour oil upon My true shepherds. Many of these are now considered the least of their brethren, but you will find them serving as faithful shepherds of their little flocks, faithful laborers in whatever I have given them to do. These are My faithful ones who are called to be kings. These I will trust with My authority. They will prepare My people for the great battle at the end."*

I then wondered in my heart, If we are now in the condition of the third group, what was to be done with the generals who did not seem to be real generals at all?

*"You are right, they are not real generals,"* the Lord answered. *"I did not appoint them, but they appointed themselves. Even so, some of them will be changed and I will make them generals. Others will become useful officers. However, most will flee at the first sight of battle, and you will not see them again.*

*"Remember this: At one time everyone in the first two groups was a part of the last one. When you go with the message of Zipporah*

*declaring that I will no longer tolerate the carnality of My people, those whom I have truly called and are devoted to obeying Me will not run from My circumcision but will stand against the carnality in the camp so that I will not have to bring judgment upon them. My shepherds are responsible for the condition of My sheep. My generals are responsible for the condition of My soldiers. Those whom I have called will take this responsibility because they love Me, they love My people, and they love righteousness."*

## Captain of the Host

Then I was no longer before the Judgment Seat, but on the mountain overlooking the army again. Wisdom was standing beside me. He was resolute, but I no longer felt the pain and anger that I did before.

*"I have allowed you see a little into the future,"* Wisdom began. *"I am sending you to those who are called to prepare My army and lead it. These are the ones who have been fighting the battle on the mountain. These are the ones who have met the army of the accuser and remained faithful. These are the ones who have watched over My people and protected them at the risk of their own lives. They are called to be leaders in My army who will fight in the great battle at the end and will stand without fear against all of the powers of darkness.*

*"As you can see, this army is marching, but there will be times when it camps. The camping is as important as the marching. It is*

*the time for planning, training and sharpening skills and weapons. It is also time for those in the first group to walk among the second and for the leaders of the second group to walk among the third group, finding those who can be called to the next level. Do this while you can, for the time is near when Revelation 11:1-2 will be fulfilled, and those who want to be called by My name but do not walk in My ways will be trodden underfoot. Before the last great battle, My army will be holy, even as I am holy. I will remove those who are not circumcised of heart and the leaders who do not uphold My righteousness. When the last battle is fought, there will be no third group as you see here.*

*"Until now when My army has camped, most of the time has been wasted. Just as I only lead My people forward with a clear objective, so it is that when I call My army to camp, there is a purpose. The strength of the army that marches will be determined by the quality of its camp. When it is time to stop and camp for a season, it is to teach My people My ways. An army is an army whether it is in battle or at peace. You must learn how to camp, how to march, and how to fight. You will not do any one of these well unless you do them all well.*

*"My army must be ready to do each of these in season and out of season. You may think that it is time to march, but I will direct you to camp because I see things that you can never see, even from this place of vision. If you follow me, you will always be doing the*

right thing at the right time, even though it may not seem right to you. Remember, I am the Captain of the Host.

"An army's resolve will be determined by the nobility of their mission, how well they are prepared for their mission, and how well they are led. This army will march with the most noble mission that has ever been given to man. However, few of My people are being equipped for their mission, and those who are now leading My people follow their own desires. I will now raise up leaders who will train and equip My people. These will always follow Me because I am the Captain of the Host.

"Many armies experience both victories and defeats. My army has been marching for many centuries. It, too, has had many victories and many defeats. My army has lost many battles because it attacked the enemy when I did not give the command. Others were defeated because they attacked the enemy with untrained people. Most of these leaders have done this because they were seeking their own glory. As Paul wrote of those in his own time, 'They all seek after their own interests.'

"Other leaders have had My interests at heart and sincerely sought a victory over evil for My name's sake, but they did not train their people well; they did not walk with Me as their Wisdom. That will now change. I will be the Captain of the Host. Do not be discouraged by the way My people now appear, but remember what they will become. I will now raise up leaders who will only march when I give the orders. When My army follows Me, it will win every *battle. When they camp, they will know My presence, and they will grow strong in My ways.*

*"You will come to a time in the future when you see My army exactly as it is now. At that time, you will feel My burning anger. Know that I will no longer abide those who remain in the condition of the third group. Then I will stop the march of the entire army until those in this group have been disciplined to become soldiers or dispersed. I will discipline those in the second group to cast off their evil ambitions and live for Me and My Truth. Then My army will march forth, not to destroy, but to give life. I will be in the midst of them to tread My enemies under this army's feet. I am coming to be the Captain of the Host!"*

# CHAPTER XI

# the city

I then stood upon another mountain looking out over a city. The glory of this city was beyond anything I had seen or imagined before. While every building and home was unique and beautiful, each fit into a breathtaking, overall symmetry with one another and the surrounding fields, mountains and bodies of water. It was almost as if the city grew like a plant instead of being built. I felt that I was looking at something that had been built by a race that had not fallen and had walked in the righteousness and purity of Adam and Eve in the beginning.

One feature that stood out was the large amount of glass windows in each structure or dwelling. This glass was so clear and clean, and the windows and doors were so situated that I sensed that I was not only welcome in each dwelling, but invited. It was also as if nothing was hidden, and there was no danger of anything being stolen.

Then I looked at the people in the city. They seemed familiar, but at the same time I knew that I had never met anyone like them. They were like I imagined Adam to be before the fall. The eyes of each one shone with what seemed to be almost total comprehension, an intellectual depth far beyond even the most brilliant person I had ever known. I knew this to be the result of an order and peace that was completely free of confusion or doubt, or maybe the confusion *of* doubt. There was no ambition because each one was so confident and had so much joy in who they were and what they were doing. Because everyone here was free, they were also completely open. Poverty or sickness seemed incomprehensible.

I looked at the streets in this city. There were many major highways in the center all going in the same direction, and many smaller roads connected these great highways. As I looked at one of the largest of the highways, knowledge was imparted to me about the truth of holiness. I looked at another highway and knew the truth about healing. As I looked at another, I began to understand things about judgment. Looking at each street, I understood a different truth. I then realized that each highway was a path to that truth. The people walking and living on each one seemed to reflect the truth of that highway.

My attention turned to the many streets connecting the highways. As I looked at each of these, I felt an impartation of a fruit of the Spirit, such as love, joy, peace or patience. These came as feelings instead of the understanding that came when I looked at the highways.

I noticed that while some of these streets were connected to every highway, some of the highways only had one or two streets connected to them. For example, I could only get to the Highway of Holiness by walking on the street of Love. I could only get to the Highway of Judgment by walking on the streets of Love or Joy. However, the Highway of Grace was joined by *all* of the streets. To get on any of the Highways of Truth, I had to walk on a street named after a fruit of the Spirit.

People were walking on the highways and streets, while some were sitting on the edges of them. Some were in the houses on a street or highway, and others were building houses on them. Those living in the houses were constantly serving food and drink to those who were walking or sitting. I then noticed that there were no restaurants, hotels or hospitals in the city. I quickly understood that none of these were needed because every home was a center of hospitality and healing.

Almost every home was open to the travelers. Those that were not open were used for special purposes, such as study or long-term healing. I wondered why anyone would even need healing here, but later I would be shown the reason. Even so, I could not imagine a more wonderful place for this great ministry of hospitality, helps or healing, even those being built on the Highway of Judgment, which seemed to be the place of the most activity. Because of this, even the Highway of Judgment was appealing. It was apparent that every street was not only safe, but was more desirable than any other road or highway I had ever seen, even in theme parks. This city was far more glorious than any utopia of which philosophers could conceive.

My attention was drawn back to the Highway of Judgment. It seemed to have been the least traveled highway, but now was becoming much more active. I then saw that this was because the other streets and highways all flowed toward this one. However, even though the Highway of Judgment was becoming the center of activity, people still seemed hesitant to enter it.

As I looked toward the end of the highway, I could see that the road was on a steady incline, and there was a high mountain at the end which was enveloped in a subtle, but profound, glory. I knew that if people could see the end of this road, there would have been far more traveling on it. I then realized that I was drawn to this road because it had the same feeling to it as the Great Hall of Judgment. I knew that this was the road that led to knowing the Lord as the Righteous Judge.

## The Bond of Peace

I wondered if this city was heaven or the New Jerusalem. Then I observed that even though these people were of stature far beyond any I had seen on earth, they did not have the glory or stature of those in even the lowest positions in the Hall of Judgment. I was wondering about this when I felt Wisdom standing next to me again.

*"These are the same people who you saw in My army,"* He began. *"The city and the army are the same. My coming leaders have had visions of both My army and My city. I am building both, and I will use the leaders I am now preparing to complete what I began generations ago. My generals will become master-builders for My city, and My master builders will also become generals. These are the same.*

*"One day, the army will no longer be needed, but this city will last forever. You must prepare the army for its present battles, but build all that you build for the future.*

*"There is a future for the earth. After My judgments have come, it will be a glorious future. I am about to show My people the future so that the future will be in their hearts. As Solomon wrote, 'Everything God does will remain forever.' As My people become like Me, they will build that which will last. They will do all that they do with a peace for the present times and a vision for the future. The city that I am building to last forever is built on truth in the*

157

*hearts of men. My truth will endure, and those who walk in truth will leave fruit that will remain.*

*"I am coming to earth in My people as Wisdom to build My city. The knowledge of truth will fill My city, but wisdom will build it. The wisdom that is coming upon My builders will cause the world to marvel at My city even more than it marveled at the city that Solomon built. Men have worshiped their own wisdom since they first ate of the Tree of Knowledge. The world's wisdom is about to pale before My wisdom which I will reveal through My city. Then those who worship any other wisdom will be ashamed. All that Solomon did was a prophecy of what I am about to build.*

*"In all that you have seen of the city that I am building, I have only given you a superficial glimpse. From time to time, you will be shown more, but for now you must see one thing. What did you notice the most about this city?"*

"The one thing that stood out the most to me was the harmony. Everything in the city fit so perfectly together, and the whole city fit so perfectly in its environment," I responded.

*"The perfect bond of peace is love,"* the Lord continued. *"In My city, there will be unity. In all that I created, there was harmony. All things fit together in Me. Everything that I am doing in the earth is to restore the original harmony between My Father and His creation and among all creatures. When mankind lives in harmony with Me, the earth will be in harmony with Him, and there will*

*be no more earthquakes, floods or storms. I came to bring peace on earth."*

As He spoke, I knew I was looking into the future, just as I had looked when I viewed the army. I also knew that what He had said about building with peace in the present and a vision for the future was also essential for the harmony I saw. Time was also a part of His creation within which we had to fit.

Wisdom then turned me so that I looked directly into His eyes and said, *"I love My creation. I love the beasts of the field and the fish of the sea. I will restore all things as they were intended to be, but I must first restore mankind. I did not come just to redeem, but to restore. To be a part of My ministry of restoration you must not just see others as they are, but as they are to become. Like Ezekiel, you must see in even the driest bones an exceedingly great army. You must prophesy life to the bones until they become the army that I have called them to be. Then My army will march. When My army marches, it will restore—not destroy. It will fight evil, but it will also build the city of righteousness.*

*"All of the treasures of the earth cannot weigh in the balance with the value of a single soul. I am building My city in the hearts of men, with the hearts of men. Those who keep the great wisdom— the knowledge of the eternal treasures—will be used to build My city. You will know My builders by this wisdom—they do not set their minds on earthly things, but on the treasures of heaven. Because*

of this, the world will bring its wealth to My city just as they did in the times of Solomon.

"I am about to release My wise master builders. You must walk with them, and they must all walk together. Each of the highways and streets that you saw in this city will begin as a fortress of truth in the earth. Each fortress will stand against the powers of darkness, and those powers will not be able to stand against them. Each will be like a mountain, with rivers flowing from it to water the earth. Each will be a city of refuge and a haven for all who seek Me. No weapon that is formed against them will prosper, and no weapon that I give to them will fail."

## The Lord's Builders

As Wisdom spoke, my eyes were opened to see the most beautiful valley I had ever seen. The mountains forming the valley and the valley, itself, were more green than any green I could remember having seen. The rocks were like fortresses made of silver; the trees were perfect and full. There was a river in the middle fed by streams flowing from every mountain around it. The water sparkled with a blue that was the bluest tint I had ever seen and beautifully matched the sky. Every blade of grass was perfect. The valley was filled with many kinds of animals which all seemed to be the very best of their breed with no diseases or scars. They fit perfectly with the valley and with one another. I had never seen such a desirable place on earth.

I wondered if I was seeing the Garden of Eden, and then I saw a few soldiers in full armor who were surveying the valley. Other soldiers were following each stream to the river, and then following the river to the place where the first soldiers were surveying. At first I did not think that the soldiers fit in this place at all, but for some reason I was quickly at ease with them because I somehow knew they were supposed to be there.

I looked at the soldiers. They were rough and battle-hardened, yet kind and approachable. They were fierce and resolute, yet seemed to be at perfect peace. They were serious and sober, yet full of joy and quick to laugh. I thought that even though war is always terrible, if I had to go to battle, there was no other group of soldiers beside whom I would rather fight.

I noticed their armor which seemed to have been custom made just for them, fitting so perfectly that they moved with a grace as though they were not wearing any armor at all. I could tell that it was both lighter, yet stronger than any I had ever seen. The armor also seemed to be a perfect combination of the colors of the water, mountains and blue sky, which I soon realized was the reflection of these colors in a purity I had never before seen in a reflection. The armor itself was of an "other-worldly" silver, deeper and purer than any silver on earth. As I was wondering who these soldiers were, the Lord began to speak.

*"In My Father's house are many dwelling places,"* He replied. *"These are My builders. Each of My houses will be a fortress from which I will send out My armies. Some will go forth as knights to fight for the poor and oppressed, while others will go forth as small companies who will raid the strongholds of the enemy and bring back the spoils. Some will send forth a host to conquer cities over which My truth and righteousness will reign, and others will join with armies from other fortresses to liberate whole nations with My truth, My love and My power.*

*"These fortresses are not just for the protection of My people, but for mobilizing, training and sending forth My army throughout the earth. The darkest of times will soon come, but My people will not be found hiding. They will go forth to conquer evil with good. They will conquer by not loving their lives even unto death and by loving others more than their own lives. These will be the fearless ones whom I will send forth before I return.*

*"Even the prophecies of their coming strike terror into the hearts of My enemies. They will have no fear. They will love. Love is more powerful than fear, and their love will break the power of fear that has held mankind in bondage since the beginning. Because they have chosen to die daily, the fear of death has no power over them. This will give them power over every enemy whose power is fear. I was once dead, but now am alive forever, and those who know Me*

cannot fear death. *Therefore, those who know Me will follow Me wherever I go.*

*"Each of My dwelling places will be in a valley like this. It is alive with the life that was in the earth before the fall because here the power of My redemption has brought forth true life again. My dwelling places will only be found where all of My streams flow together into one. My builders will come from every stream, but they will work as one. Just as great houses need different craftsmen, so does My house. Only when they work together can they build My house.*

*"As you see in these, My builders will have the wisdom to complete the survey before they build. Each of My houses will fit perfectly into the land where they are located, not according to human measurements, but according to Mine. The first skill that My builders develop is the skill of surveying. They must know the land because I designed the land for My people. When you build with My wisdom, what you build will fit perfectly with the land."*

Then I was standing by one of the streams in the valley. I started following it to the top of a mountain. As I got close to the top, I began to hear loud, terrible sounds. When I looked beyond the valley, I could see wars and great earthquakes tearing the earth, and storms and fires that seemed to completely encircle the valley. It was as if I was standing on the border between heaven and hell, looking into hell itself. I somehow knew that all of hell was powerless to encroach on the valley, but the sight was so terrible, I turned to run back into the valley. I then felt Wisdom standing beside me.

*"This is where you must live, between the dying and the living. Do not fear, but believe. You have been weak, but now I am with you, so be courageous and strong. Fear must not rule over you—do nothing because of fear. Do what you do because of love, and you will always triumph. Love is the source of courage. Love will prevail in the end. Encourage My builders with these words."*

# Chapter XII

# Words of Life

Then I was back at the Great Hall of Judgment, standing before the same door again. I was still a little stunned by what I had seen on the edge of the valley, but His words were still resounding in me. "Love, love," I repeated over and over. "I must not forget the power of love. There is perfect peace in love. There is courage in love. There is power in love."

I looked at the door. I knew that this was the door to His church. I knew that the fortresses that Wisdom talked about were churches and movements. I began to think of some congregations and movements which I knew were already preparing for what I had seen. I began thinking of spiritual surveyors whom I knew but had never thought of in this way before. Then again, it seemed like most of them were so battle-weary that they were just trying to survive, even fighting one another in their desperation.

I thought of the battle that had been fought on the mountain. The enemy had used Christians to attack other Christians who were trying to climb the mountain. Even though that battle was eventually won and most of the Christians freed from the accuser's power, I knew that it would take a long time for the wounds from those battles to heal. Many had been under the influence of the accuser for so long that it was still a part of their nature to accuse, and it could be a while before their minds were renewed. I knew that the church was still a very long way from being united.

Where do we begin? I thought to myself. What can I do if I go through that door?

*"You do not have to begin. It is already finished,"* Wisdom answered. *"I accomplished the unity of My people on the cross. Even though it looks like the enemy has prevailed since the cross, he actually only has worked into the plan which My Father and I had from the beginning. When you preach the cross and live by its power, you will do My will. Those who serve Me and not their own ambitions will soon recognize one another and be joined together. Those who have the true fear of God do not have to fear anything on the earth. Those who fear Me will not fear one another, but will love each other and sit together at My table.*

*"I have called you to see, and you will see how My kingdom will come. The devil will be cast down to the earth and will come to the earth with great wrath. But do not fear his wrath, for I am also about to show My wrath against all iniquity. The evil one and*

*all who follow evil will soon know My wrath. You must see these things, but you are not to fear them because I dwell in the midst of My people and am greater than all. As you behold Me you will not fear. If you fear, it is because you are not beholding Me.*

*"When the evil in mankind has become fully united with the evil one, the great time of trouble will come upon the earth. Then all of mankind and the whole creation will understand the futility and tragedy of rebellion. At the same time, My people will become fully united with Me, and My great light will stand against the great darkness. Those who walk in lawlessness will fall into the deep darkness. Those who walk in obedience will shine forth as the stars of heaven.*

*"Humility and obedience will always lead to Me. As you come to Me, you will behold and manifest My glory. The heavens and the earth are about to behold the difference between the light and the darkness. You are called to live between the darkness and the light, in order to call those who live in darkness to the light. Even now I do not desire for any to perish."*

In the glory that surrounded us, it was difficult to remember the darkness and terrible events that I had just witnessed. I thought of the difference between His glory and even the greatest pomp and splendor of man. "How pitifully insignificant we are!" I blurted out. "If all of mankind could just have a glimpse of Your Judgment Seat they would all quickly repent. Lord, why do You not just show Yourself to the world so it will not have to endure this evil? No one would choose evil if they could see You as You are."

*"I will reveal Myself. When evil has run its full course, then I will show Myself to the world. As the evil one is being revealed through fallen men, I will be revealed through restored men. Then the world will see Me—not just the glory that I have in heaven, but as My glory stands against the darkness. My glory is more than what you see here; it is My nature. After I reveal My nature in My people, I will return in the glory that I have here. Until then, I am seeking those who will follow Me because they love Me and love the truth, not just because they love this glory and power.*

*"Those who choose to obey when the whole world is disobeying are worthy to be heirs with Me. These will be worthy to rule with Me, to see My glory, and to share it. These are the ones who do not live for themselves, but for Me. Some of the greatest of these brethren of mine are about to be revealed. They will stand for truth against the greatest darkness. They will remain steadfast through the greatest trials. I have brought you here, and I am sending you back to encourage them to stand and not faint for the time of their salvation is near.*

*"I am also sending you back to warn these mighty ones. Satan saw the glory of My Father and beheld the myriads who serve Him, yet he still fell. He fell because he started to trust in the glory and power that the Father had shared with him instead of trusting the Father. Those who will be entrusted with the power and glory I share with them in these times must not put their trust in the power*

or glory, but in Me. *True faith is never in yourself, your wisdom or the power that I have given to you. True faith is in Me.*

*"As you grow in the true faith that is in Me, you will grow in dependence on Me, and you will trust yourself less. Those who begin to trust in themselves will not be able to carry the weight of My power or glory; they can fall just as the evil one did. My strength is made perfect in weakness, but you must never forget that in yourself you are weak, and by yourself you are foolish.*

*"Those who are worthy to reign with Me in the age to come will prove this by living in the darkness and weakness of human flesh, yet they will serve and trust Me. Even the greatest angels will gladly bow before those who have been proven in this way. The angels marvel when suffering men and women who have beheld so little of the glory here remain steadfast for Me and My truth in times of darkness. These are worthy to be called My brethren and to be called the sons and daughters of My Father.*

*"On earth, the truth often looks weak and easily defeated. Those who see from here know that My truth always prevails. The time when I stand up and bring My judgments to the earth has only been delayed so that My brethren could prove their love for Me by standing for truth at any cost. My truth and My goodness will prevail for all of eternity, and so will all who come to Me because they love the truth. These will shine forth as the stars which were made in honor of them."*

As Wisdom continued to speak, it was like being washed in a shower of living water. At times I had been ashamed because even in the presence of His glory, I was as dull and easily distracted here as I was on earth. But now as He spoke to me, His words cleansed me so that a sharpness came to my mind beyond just mental exhilaration. The more I was cleansed, the more His words seemed to explode with cleansing brilliance. I not only saw His glory, but *felt* His glory inside of me. In His presence, I did not just hear the truth, I *absorbed* the truth.

## His Beloved Bride

This sensation of being cleansed by His words was more wonderful than can be described, but it was familiar. I knew that I had felt this when listening to anointed preaching from one who had been in the presence of the Lord. It was not intoxicating, but the exact opposite. Instead of dulling the senses, it quickened them. In His presence, I felt that thousands of fragments of information which I had accumulated over the years were all tied together to give a deep and comprehensive meaning to everything He said. In this way, every concept became like a strong pillar of knowledge in my mind. Then it became a passion as I felt a deep love for each truth.

When He spoke, there was an energy released that enabled me to see each truth with a greater depth than ever before. His words did not just impart information, but *life*. This great illumination was similar to what I experienced after I decided not to try and hide anything when I was standing in front of the Judgment Seat. The more I opened my heart to His words to expose any darkness in me and to change me, the more power His words seemed to have in me.

The Lord did not just give information when He spoke, but somehow rearranged my mind and heart so that these truths would be the foundation for understanding, and the understanding released a love for the truth. For example, I had what I thought was a sound understanding of the church as the bride of Christ. As He talked about the ministries being sent forth to prepare His bride, I saw in my heart what seemed to be every church I knew. They immediately became much more than just a group of people; they became *His Beloved.* I felt a burning passion to help them prepare for Him. The repulsion of sin and harlotry with the world almost buckled my knees as I saw what it did to His people. I knew that I was feeling what He was feeling.

His cleansing truth poured over me. The cleanness I felt was more wonderful than I had ever believed possible. It was almost as if I had been living my life in a sewer and was now being given a hot shower. The power of cleansing truth gripped me so powerfully that I desperately wanted to carry it back to share with His people.

*"I am about to release the power of anointed truth to cleanse My people,"* Wisdom continued. *"My bride will be cleansed of all of her defilements. I am sending forth My messengers who will*

*be flames of fire, burning with zeal for My holiness and the holiness of My people."*

As He spoke, I felt the depth and power of the message of holiness. I then knew without question the power of truth to accomplish this. A vision of the glorious bride whom He so deserves was burned into my heart. I passionately wanted to share this with His people so that they would become completely focused on getting ready for Him. I just could not comprehend doing anything again without this being my purpose.

He began to speak about the fortresses of truth and righteousness. While He talked, I saw the congregations with whom I was familiar and how they were struggling. I became burdened as never before for them to be empowered with His truth. I knew that they were weak because they were not walking in truth. The grief that I felt for them became almost more than I could bear.

"Why do they not walk in truth?" I blurted out.

*"You are beginning to feel the burden that Nehemiah felt when he heard that Jerusalem was in distress because her walls were broken down,"* Wisdom explained. *"I am imparting to My messengers the fire to see My bride cleansed, and I am also imparting to them the burden of Nehemiah to see the walls of salvation restored. Then My people will no longer be in distress.*

*"You have seen My people as My army, My city and My bride. Now you do not just see these, but you feel them. Only when My truth comes from the heart does it have the power to change men. Living waters must come from the innermost being—the heart. Just as you felt My truth cleansing you, I am making My messengers flames of fire who will speak truth, not to just give understanding, but with the power to change men's hearts. The truth that I am sending will not just convict My people of their sin, but will cleanse them from their sin."*

Even as He was speaking, a great zeal rose up within me to do something. Divine strategies began coming to me which I knew could help His people. I could not wait to begin. I now believed that even the driest bones were going to become an exceedingly great army! In the presence of Wisdom, nothing seemed impossible. I had no trouble believing that His church would become a bride without spot or wrinkle, or that His church would become a great city, standing as a fortress of truth for the whole world to behold. I had no doubt that His people, even as weak and defeated as they now seemed, were about to become an army of truth before which no power of darkness could stand. Feeling the power of truth as never before, I knew that His power was much greater than the darkness.

## Words of Life

In His presence, I felt as if I could speak forth the vision I had received of His bride and whoever heard it be changed. It seemed that I could speak to the most defeated little congregation with such power that they would quickly become a mighty fortress of truth. I also knew that on earth, my words did not have that power.

*"Your words will have this power when you abide in Me,"* Wisdom interjected. *"I did not call you to preach about Me; I called you to be a voice that I could speak through. As you abide in Me and My words abide in you, you will bear fruit that will remain. By My word, the creation was brought forth, and by My word the new creation will come forth in you and in My people. My words are Spirit and Life. My words give Life. You are not called to just teach about Me, but to let Me teach through you. As you dwell in My presence, your words will be My words, and they will have power."*

I thought of something that Margaret Browning had once said: "Every bush is aflame with the fire of God, but only those who see take off their shoes. The rest just pick the berries."

"Lord, I want to see you in everything," I said.

*"I will give My messengers the vision to see My purpose in all things,"* He responded. *"I will make My messengers flames of fire such as I appeared at the burning bush. My fire will rest upon them, but they will not be consumed by it. Then mankind will marvel at*

*this great sight and turn aside to see it. I will speak from the midst of My messengers, calling My people to their destiny and to rise up as the deliverers that I have called them to be."*

I then felt drawn to the door. I stepped closer to it and could see writing. I had never seen writing like this before. It was of the purest gold, and somehow it was alive. I began to read.

**For by Him all things were created, in the heavens and on earth, visible and invisible, whether thrones or dominions or rulers or authorities—all things have been created by Him and for Him.**

**And He is before all things, and in Him all things hold together.**

**He is also head of the body, the church; and He is the beginning, the first-born from the dead; so that He Himself might come to have first place in everything.**

**For it was the Father's good pleasure for all the fulness to dwell in Him,**

**and through Him to reconcile all things to Himself, having made peace through the blood of His cross; through Him, whether things on earth or things in heaven.**

**And although you were formerly alienated and hostile in mind, engaged in evil deeds,**

yet He has now reconciled you in His fleshly body through death, in order to present you before Him holy and blameless and beyond reproach—

if indeed you continue in the faith firmly established and steadfast, and not moved away from the hope of the gospel that you have heard, which was proclaimed in all creation under heaven, and of which I, Paul, was made a minister.

Now I rejoice in my sufferings for your sake, and in my flesh I do my share on behalf of His body, which is the church, in filling up that which is lacking in Christ's afflictions.

Of this church I was made a minister according to the stewardship from God bestowed on me for your benefit, that I might fully carry out the word of God,

that is the mystery which has been hidden from the past ages and generations; but has now been manifested to His saints,

to whom God willed to make known what is the riches of the glory of this mystery among the Gentiles, which is Christ in you, the hope of glory.

And we proclaim Him, admonishing every man and teaching every man with all wisdom, that we may present every man complete in Christ.

**And for this purpose also I labor, striving according to His power, which mightily works within me (Colossians 1:16-29).**

As I read these words, they were like a transfusion of life. A single word from God is worth more than all of the treasure on earth! I thought, How could I ever allow myself to be so carried away with the cares of the world when I have His words? I began to think about how worthwhile it would be to cross the earth to hear just one anointed sermon, but sometimes I was so lazy that I did not want to drive across town. I was appalled at my carelessness with His Word as I stood before the door. "Lord, I am so sorry," I blurted out.

As I said this, the door opened. As it did, I pondered how it had looked so dull and uninviting from a distance, but up close it was more intricate and beautiful than any door I had ever seen. That is how people judge the church, I thought, and how I have often judged it myself. I have loved God for a long time, but failed to love His people the way that I should.

*"Such repentance will open the door for you to go forth into the purpose for which I called you. You cannot fulfill your purpose apart from My people. I have called My people to be one, and now it will come to pass. Apart from them, you cannot live what you have seen in your visions. Now you must go from seeing the way and knowing the truth to being a vessel for My life. This you cannot do apart from My people. The Father has given you His love for Me, that His love might be in you, just as I asked. Now I will give you My love for*

*My people. My messengers must see them as I do and love them as*
*I do. As you truly love My word, the door to your destiny with My*
*people will open for you."*

His words did not just touch my mind, but also my heart.
I felt each one. Just hearing the love with which He spoke of
His people imparted that love to me. This was a greater love
than I had ever felt before, but it was also familiar and I had
experienced it to a degree when I had heard anointed
preaching. I thought about how in my foolishness, I had often
said that there would be no preaching in heaven, but now I
felt that it could not be heaven without preaching. I began to
even crave the preaching of His word.

*"Yes there will be preaching and teaching in heaven. For all*
*of eternity, My story will be told. That is why it is called the eternal*
*gospel. I am the Word and I am Truth, and words of truth will*
*forever fill My creation. All of creation will delight in My words of*
*truth just as you are now. Even the angels love to listen to your*
*testimonies, and they will hear them. My redeemed ones will forever*
*love to tell and listen to the stories of My redemption. But now you*
*must tell them to those who dwell in darkness. The word of your*
*testimony will liberate many. Those who love Me love My word.*
*They love to read it and they love to hear it. You have been given*
*the truth that will set men free, which is My word in your heart. Go*
*forth with My word. Go forth and you will see the power of My word."*

# CHAPTER XIII

# the manna

I stepped through the door. When I did, I was surprised that all of the glory in which I had been standing before was gone. It was dark and musty, like an old cellar. It was disconcerting, but I still felt the power of the words that the Lord had spoken to me, and they steadied me.

"What you feel is the anointing of the Holy Spirit," a voice said from the darkness.

"Who are you?" I asked.

"Must you ask?" It did not quite sound like Wisdom, but some other familiar voice. Even so, I knew that it was Him. Gradually, my eyes adjusted to the darkness and I was surprised to see my old friend, the white eagle.

"He lives in you, and so you can abide in all that you just experienced here just as you did in His presence there. I know that you have become addicted to His presence, and this is right, but here you must learn to recognize Him in many forms. First you must recognize His voice in your own heart and then as He speaks through others.

"This you have known before, and have experienced from time to time, but not like you must know it now. He will never be far from you and can always be found easily. He will always lead you to the truth. Only by the Holy Spirit can you see and know anything or anyone the way they really are. In the times that are before us, we will perish if we do not follow Him closely." *lead by the Spirit, or else ~me 2*

"I know that this is true because I hear Wisdom speaking through you. Are you here to show me the way? I can hardly see here."

"I will come to you from time to time to tell you about the signposts that will let you know that you are still on the right path, but the Holy Spirit must lead you. I will also help you to understand how He leads you in different places, but first I must tell you about the manna so that you can live."

"Manna! Do you mean like the manna that Israel ate in the wilderness? Is that what we eat here?"

"It is what all who have walked with God have lived on since the beginning. The manna that Israel ate while in the wilderness was a prophecy of this. The Lord will give you fresh manna daily. Just as He covered the earth with manna every day for Israel while they were in the wilderness, He covers the earth each day with truth for His people. Every way that you turn, you will see it. Even in the midst of the darkness and gloom, His Word will surround you, and you can gather it. Those who are cast into the inner prisons will awake to find it every day. Those who live in great palaces can also find it every day. But His manna is as gentle and light as the dew, and easily trampled. You must be gentle and light of heart to see it."

## Living Epistles

"The Lord speaks every day to each one of His people. They cannot live by bread alone, but must have the words that proceed from His mouth. These are not the words that He spoke in the past, but the words that He speaks to them each day," the eagle continued.

"Many are weak because they do not know how to gather the manna that the Lord gives to them each day. They go astray because they do not know His voice. His sheep know His voice, and they follow Him because they recognize it. The manna is the bread of life that each of His people is given each day. You must learn to recognize it, and help His people to recognize this manna. When they taste it as you are tasting it now, they will diligently search for it each day. Do not be concerned about hoarding food or water, but learn to see and partake of the manna that He gives daily. This will preserve you when all else fails.

"The Scriptures are the meat that the Lord gives to us, but His manna is found in His living epistles, His people. He will speak to you each day through His people. You must open your heart to the way that He is found in His people if you are to partake of the heavenly manna. Just as He said to Jerusalem, He is saying to us, "You shall not see Me until you say, 'Blessed is He who comes in the name of the Lord!'" This spoke of Him when He walked the earth then, and it speaks of the way that He is walking the earth now through His people. As our love for manna grows, so will our love for each other. If you are growing in love, the manna which He serves will never taste old or stale to you, but will be new each morning.

"His manna may come to you through the words of a close friend or one of His people who lived long before you as you ponder their writings. He will also speak through those who do not know Him, but you will know that He sent them to you. You will discern His manna when you go beyond just trying to hear His words and seek to hear the Word, Himself. It is not just hearing His words, but hearing His voice that will lead you in the way in which you are to go. Many repeat the words that He has spoken, but His manna is the word that He is speaking now.

"We need the strong meat of the Scriptures to build ourselves up and give us the container for gathering His manna. Grow strong on the meat of His written Word, but also develop a taste for His manna. The meat of His written Word will build us up and prepare us for what is to come, but manna will sustain us through what lies ahead.

"The words that were spoken to you through the saints in the Hall of Judgment were manna from Him. His people are also His manna to the world. Manna is the bread of life—the living words which He speaks to His people daily and are spoken through His people. The Scriptures are set and cannot be changed. They are the anchor for our souls. However, the Book of Life is still being written. He writes a new chapter in the Book of Life with each soul that comes to Him."

## Victory or Defeat

"The Scriptures are the blueprint for His dwelling place that He is building among men. They are the testimony of the way that He has worked through men and women to bring about their redemption. His people are the vessels of His living word and are witnesses to the world that His words are not just history, but are still alive and still give life. If you are to know His words, you must know both the Scripture *and* His manna. The Scriptures are His eternal plans that will not change which we must know to walk in His ways. His manna will give you the strength to walk each day. This is so that we might have fellowship. 'If we walk in the light as He Himself is in the light, we have fellowship with one another,'" the eagle said.

"Many of His messengers do not even know that they are being used in this way. They often do not know when He is speaking through them. Those to whom He is speaking seldom recognize His voice. This must change. His people are called to be in unity with Him in all that He does, but few even know His voice. Therefore they seldom follow Him in the way that He wants to lead them. He now wants all of His people to know when He is speaking through them or to them. Just as the sure communication between a general and his soldiers can determine the outcome of the battle, the strength of His communication with His people will determine their victory or defeat in the days to come.

"He is now preparing many messengers who will go forth with His messages. They will also teach His people to know His voice and to know His ways. You must receive His messengers as if you are receiving the Lord, Himself. You must help them along their way. The success of their ministry will determine the rise and fall of many."

For a moment I thought that if the Lord was sending them, surely they would not need my help. This brought a stern rebuke from the eagle, who could also discern my thoughts.

"Do not think that way! Many of His people fall because of that delusion! He could do all things without us, but He has chosen to do them through us. We are His provision for one another. He sent the Helper to live in His people;

therefore, He intends for His people to receive their help through one another. Do not ever forget this. That is why He gives us our manna through one another. He has designed all things so that we must love Him above all things, but we must also love one another. We need Him above all things, but we also need each other. In this way, we are also kept humble so that He might trust us with His grace and power."

"I'm sorry," I replied. "I know all of that very well, but I tend to forget it at times."

"The times that you have forgotten this have been more costly than you need to know at this time, but to forget this in the future will be more costly than you can bear. We need the Lord above all, but we also need all of His people. It is in His people that we will find the Helper, the One who leads us into all truth and the One who leads us to the Son.

"He is now sending forth His messengers. Some will be old and wise. Others will be young and have little experience, but they will know His voice. The enemy will also be sending his messengers to sow confusion. This, too, is a part of our training. Some will be deceived by the messengers of the enemy for a while, and others will suffer loss because of them, but those who love the Lord and His truth will not be deceived by them for long. Those who love Him and His truth will know the truth. Those who have been deceived for a time will learn from this, and they will be used to expose the deceivers in the days to come.

"Some who have been the most deceived in the past will become some of the strongest in the truth because of their wisdom. Wisdom is to know His voice and to follow Him. These will not be easily distracted from Him again. Do not judge others because of their past, but by who they have become. Those who have followed Wisdom will have their weaknesses turned into strengths. No one is stronger or more trustworthy than those who know His voice and follow Him.

"We must not stop encouraging His people to know His voice. We must charge His prophets to confront and expose the false prophets. This message we must carry to the end. We are being sent to help build His lines of communication with those who will be His soldiers in the great battle to come. *All* of His people must know His voice. The time will soon be upon us when all who do not know His voice will be deceived by the darkness. Those who know His voice because they know Him will not be deceived."

As the eagle spoke, his words continued to wash me just as they had when they came in the presence of Wisdom. I could not see Him, but I knew that He was present and that He was the One speaking to me. Though I could not see as much with my eyes in this place, I had great clarity of mind that enabled me to understand. I had always felt that I had a very poor memory, but although He now was saying much more than He ever had before, it seemed like I could remember every word He said, even when it came through someone else. I then knew that this was the power of the Holy Spirit Who brings all things to our remembrance. In Him, looking backward or forward was no different from looking at the present. As I was thinking about this, the eagle continued.

"This place seems musty and old because very little fresh air has been let in here for a long time. You have found the door and have entered. The same door that led you to this place also can now lead you back to the Hall of Judgment. What did you receive in the Hall of Judgment?"

"Wisdom and understanding," I replied.

"In a single word, you received grace," the eagle responded. "The Throne of Judgment is also the Throne of Grace. You can boldly go there at any time."

When he said this, I turned to see the door behind me. Now I could see beauty in it that was even greater than when I entered the Hall of Judgement. I opened it and stepped through again.

# CHAPTER XIV
# the call

I looked at Wisdom, who then turned me around so that I could behold the Great Hall again. I was startled to see standing right behind me everyone whom I had previously met there. I was even more surprised by how much more glorious they now seemed.

*"They have not changed,"* Wisdom said. *"You have changed. Your eyes are opened to see more than you could before. The more clearly that you are able to see Me, the more you will be able to see Me in others."*

I looked toward the Apostle Paul. He was regal beyond description. He had such great authority and dignity, but was at the same time so graced with humility that I am sure the lowest peasant or sinner would have felt completely comfortable approaching him. The desire to be just like that flooded me.

I then looked at the others and felt as if they were all the closest family and friends I had ever known. It is impossible to describe how I loved them and how I knew that they loved me. No fellowship on earth could compare, but the best on earth was somehow a foretaste of this. There was no pretension, posturing or positioning. Everyone knew everyone else completely, and love was the source of every thought. Eternity with this family was going to be even better than I had ever imagined. I desperately wanted to take all of them with me, but I knew that they could not leave their present domain.

Wisdom again answered my thoughts, *"They will be with you as I am with you. Remember, they are the great cloud of witnesses. Even when you do not see them, they are as close to you as they are now. All who have served Me from the beginning are one body and they, too, will be with you in what is to come, but I will be in you."*

I wondered how anything that we experienced in eternity could be better than what was to be found right here in the Judgment Hall. The judgment came from every thought being made manifest. It was not a judgment of punishment, but liberation, if there was no attempt to hide anything. Freedom came with everything that was illuminated so that there was a desire for every heart flaw to be exposed. The love was so great that I knew everything would be covered and made right.

"*Everything that you feel in My presence is true,*" Wisdom continued. "*This love and closeness that you experience here with your brethren are real. You are all one in Me, and you will grow in this love as you grow in Me. As you do, this same love will help others to enter the freedom you have experienced here. When My people who now walk the earth embrace My true judgment, they will walk in a freedom that will enable Me to touch the world with My love.*

"*It is not My desire that any should perish or suffer loss when they come here. I desire for all to judge themselves so that I will not have to judge them. That is why My judgments are about to come to the earth. They are coming in ever increasing waves, so that the world may believe and repent. Each trumpet sound will be louder than the previous one. It is the job of My messengers to help the world understand the sound of the trumpets.*

"*Remember that those with whom you must walk on earth are also members of My body. They have not yet been glorified, but you must see them as they are called to be, not as they appear now. You must love them and see the authority and grace in them that you now see in these. Remember that those with whom you walk on earth now see you as you see them. You must learn not to see according to their present appearance, but see who they are to become.*

*"Only those who live by My judgments and abide with Me as their wisdom can see My authority in others. Even so, do not strive to have men see My authority in you. Do not be concerned by whether others see you as you are; only be concerned about recognizing others as they are and seeing Me in them. When you become concerned about how others see you, you lose your authority. When authority becomes your goal, you will begin to lose true authority. You know the ministry and authority that I have given to you; do not ask people to call you by your position, but by your name. Then I will make your name greater than your position.*

*"In My kingdom, authority comes from who you are, not your title. Your ministry is your function, not your rank. Here rank is earned by humility, service and love. The deacon who loves more is higher than the apostle who loves less. On earth, prophets may be used to shake the nations, but here they will be known by their love. This is also your call—to love with My love and serve with My heart. Then we will be one."*

# CHAPTER XV

# worship in spirit

As I listened to Wisdom, it was difficult to comprehend anyone, even this great cloud of witnesses, desiring authority or position in His presence. It seemed that in every moment I had spent here, He had become greater in glory and authority, and I knew that my vision of Him was still limited. Just as the universe was obviously expanding at a great pace and the vastness of it was already incomprehensible, our revelation of Him would likewise be expanding for eternity. "How could mere humans ever represent You?" I questioned.

*"When My Father moves His little finger, the whole universe trembles. To shake the nations with your words does not impress anyone who dwells here. But when even the least of My brethren on earth shows love, it brings joy to My Father's heart. When even the most humble church sings to My Father with true love in their hearts, He silences all of heaven to listen to them. He knows that one cannot help but to worship when they are beholding His glory here, but*

*when those who are living in such darkness and difficulty sing with true hearts to Him, it touches Him more than all of the myriads of heaven can.*

*"Many times, the broken notes from earth caused all of heaven to weep with joy as they beheld My Father being touched. A few holy ones struggling to express their adoration for Him has many times caused Him to weep. Every time I see My brethren touch Him with true worship, it makes the pain and grief I knew on the cross seem like a small price to pay. Nothing brings Me more joy than when you worship My Father. I went to the cross so that you could worship Him through Me. It is in this worship that you, the Father and I are all one."*

Of all that I had yet experienced, the emotion coming from the Lord as He told me this was greater than I had ever experienced. He was not weeping or laughing. His voice was steady, but what He was telling me about worship came from such depths within Him that it was almost more than I could take. I knew that I was hearing the deepest love of the Son of God—to see His Father's joy. True worship from the embattled, struggling, believers on earth could do this like nothing else could.

For the first time, I now badly wanted to leave that place, even with all of its glory, just to get into even the most dreary little worship service on earth. I was overwhelmed by the fact that we could actually touch the Father. One person who worshiped Him from earth during these dark times meant more to the Father than the millions and millions who worshiped Him in heaven. From earth we could touch His heart at this time like we might never be able to do again! I was so overtaken by this that I did not even realize I had fallen prostrate. I then fell into something like a deep sleep.

I saw the Father. Millions and millions were attending Him. His glory was so great and the power of His presence so awesome that I felt that the whole earth would not have even measured as a grain of sand before Him. When I had once heard His audible voice, I felt like an atom standing before the sun, but when I saw Him, I knew that the sun was like an atom before Him. The galaxies were like curtains around Him. His robe was composed of millions and millions of living stars. *Everything* in His presence was living—His throne, His crown, His scepter. I knew that I could dwell before Him forever and never cease to marvel; there was no higher purpose in the universe than to worship Him.

Then the Father became intent on one thing. All of heaven seemed to stop and watch. He was beholding the cross. The Son's love for His Father which He continued to express through all of the pain and darkness then coming upon Him touched the Father so deeply that He began to quake. When He did, heaven and earth quaked. When the Father closed His eyes, heaven and earth grew dark. The emotion of the

Father was so great that I did not think I could have survived if I had beheld this scene for more than the brief moment that I did.

Then I was in a different place, beholding a worship service in a little church building. As sometimes happens in a prophetic experience, I just seemed to know everything about everyone in the battered little room. All were experiencing severe trials in their lives, but they were not even thinking of them here. They were not praying about their needs. They were all trying to compose songs of thanksgiving to the Lord. They were happy, and their joy was sincere.

I saw heaven, and all of heaven was weeping. I then saw the Father again and knew why heaven was weeping. They were weeping because of the tears in the eyes of the Father. This little group of seemingly beaten down, struggling people had moved God so deeply that He wept. They were not tears of pain, but of joy. When I saw the love that He felt for these few worshipers, I could not contain my own tears.

Nothing I had experienced gripped me more than this scene. Worshiping the Lord on earth was now more desirable to me than dwelling in all of the glory of heaven. I knew that I had been given a message that could help prepare the saints for the battles that remained on earth, but now this did not mean nearly as much to me as trying to convey how we could touch the Father. Genuine adoration expressed by even the most humble believer on earth could cause all of heaven to rejoice, but even more than that, it touches the Father. This is why the angels would rather be given charge over a single believer on the earth than to be given authority over many galaxies of stars.

I saw Jesus standing next to the Father. Beholding the joy of the Father as He watched the little prayer meeting, He turned to me and said, *"This is why I went to the cross. Giving My Father joy for just one moment would have been worth it all. Your worship can cause Him joy every day. Your worship when you are in the midst of difficulties touches Him even more than all of the worship of heaven. Here, where His glory is seen, the angels cannot help but to worship. When you worship without seeing His glory in the midst of your trials, that is worship in Spirit and in truth. The Father seeks such to be His worshipers. Do not waste your trials. Worship the Father, not for what you will receive, but to bring Him joy. You will never be stronger than when you bring Him joy, for the joy of the Lord is your strength."*

# CHAPTER XVI

# the sin

Then I was standing beside Wisdom again. He did not speak for a long time, but I did not need words. I needed to let what I had just seen saturate my soul. I strove to fathom the great business that we had been given just to be the Father's worshipers. To Him, the sun was like an atom and the galaxies like grains of sand. Yet He listened to our prayers, enjoying us continually as He beheld us, and, I was sure, often grieving for us. He was much bigger than a human mind could ever conceive, but I knew that He was also the most emotional Being in the universe. We could touch God! Every human being had the power to cause Him joy or pain. I had known this theologically, but now I knew it in a way that shattered the seeming importance of everything else.

There was no way I would ever have words to convey this, but I knew that I had to spend what time I was given on earth worshiping Him. It was like a new revelation: I could actually bring God joy! I could bring Jesus joy! I understood what the Lord had meant when He said that this was why He went to the cross. Any sacrifice would be worth it to just touch His heart for the briefest of seconds. I did not want to waste another moment when I knew that it could be spent worshiping Him. It was also obvious that the greater the trials or darkness from which the worship came, the more it touched Him. It made me want to receive trials so that I could worship Him through them.

At the same time, I felt like Job when he said that although he previously had only known Him by the hearing of the ears, when he saw Him, he repented in dust and ashes. I was like Philip who had been with Jesus for so long and did not know that he was seeing the Father through Him. How astonishing our dullness must be to the angels! Then Wisdom spoke again.

*"Remember the potential for even the least of My little ones to touch the heart of the Father. That alone makes their value greater than any price. I would have gone to the cross again for a single one of these. I also feel your pain. I know your trials because we share them. I feel the pain and the joy of every soul. That is why I still intercede continually for all of you. There will be a time when all tears are wiped away from every eye. There will be a time when only joy is known again. Until then, pain can be used. Do not waste your trials. Your greatest worship and the greatest expression of your faith that pleases Us will come in the midst of your trials.*

*"You must see Me in your own heart, and you must see Me in others. You must see Me in the great and in the small. Just as I appeared differently in each of these who now stand before you, I will come to you in different people. I will come to you in different circumstances. Your highest purpose is to recognize Me, to hear My voice, and to follow Me."*

As I turned to look at Wisdom, He was not there. I looked all around. I could feel Him everywhere, but could not see Him. I then looked back at the witnesses who stood before me. He was there. I could not see Him, but in a more profound way than I had known before, He was in each of them. As the Reformer began to speak, it was his own voice, but I could hear the voice of Wisdom in him just as when He spoke to me directly.

"He has always been in us. He is in you. He is in those to whom you must return. From time to time, He will appear to you again, but you must know that when you do not see Him as He appears, you can better recognize Him where He dwells—*in* His people. He is Wisdom. He knows how, when, and through whom to speak to you. The ones through whom He speaks to you are a part of the message. Remember what He said when He wept over Jerusalem: 'From now on you shall not see Me until you say, "Blessed is he who comes in the name of the Lord."' You will not see Him unless you can see Him in those whom He sends to you."

"It is easy for me to see and hear Him in you," I replied, "but it is not nearly so easy with those on the earth who have not yet been glorified."

"It is not meant to be easy there," Angelo replied. "To search for Him is the call of the kings who will reign with Him. Those who love Him and who love the truth will search for Him more than they would for the greatest treasures or conquests."

## Conquered by Him

"The greatest calling of all is to be fully conquered by Him," a man whom I did not recognize offered, stepping toward the front. "I should know," he added, and then he told me his name. I was shocked that this man would be found in the company of the saints. He had been a great conqueror, but I had always believed that he had done more damage to the name of Christ than possibly anyone else.

"I, too, found the grace of the cross before the end of my time," he said. "You are not just going back to conquer *for* Him, but to be conquered *by* Him. If you will devote yourself to surrendering to Him, He will use you to conquer in His name. True conquest is to capture the hearts of men with the truth that sets them free. Those who follow Him more closely will be used to conquer the most and will be the greatest of kings. On the earth, these will seldom realize that they have conquered anything. They will not see what they have really accomplished until they get here. Those who lay up great treasures on earth—even treasures that may be considered spiritual—will have little here."

"On earth you cannot measure eternal treasures," Paul said. "When I died, it looked like everything for which I had given my life to building on earth had already perished. The churches I had given my life to raising up were falling into apostasy, and even some of my closest friends were turning against me. During my last days, I felt that I had been a failure."

"Yes, but even I count Paul as a spiritual father," the great conqueror continued, "as do most of us who are here. Most who will come through the great battle of the end will be victorious because he was faithful to stand for truth. You will not measure true spiritual fruit rightly while you are on the earth. You can only measure your true success by how much more clearly you are able to behold the Lord, by how much better you know His voice, and by how much more you love the brethren."

Then Paul spoke again.

"For months before my execution, I did feel like a failure. However, on the day of my execution I was reminded of Stephen who I had watched die at my own feet years before. The memory of the light that was on his face that day had carried me through many trials. I always felt that he had somehow died for me so that I could see the true light. I knew that if I died like Stephen, then even if everything else I had done had been futile, it would insure that my life would not have been in vain. I was so thankful that I really was dying for the sake of the gospel, even if it did not look then like my ministry had accomplished very much.

"As the revelation of this came upon me, so did the grace, and my last day on earth was the most wonderful of all. I then realized that as I had lived and sincerely tried to die daily to my own desires in order to serve the gospel, every time I denied myself, there were eternal seeds planted even though I could not yet see them in the temporary realm. Being here, I can now see that this is certainly true. You must not try to judge by the fruit you see on earth, but do what you must do because it is right.

"Even so, more than bearing fruit, your call must be to know the Lord. If you seek Him, you will always find Him. He is always near to those who draw near. Many want His presence, but they do not draw near. You must do more than *want* Him: You must *seek* Him. This is part of your call. There is no higher purpose. Your victory will be measured by your seeking. You will always be as close to Him as you want to be. Your victory in life will be according to your desire for Him."

Then Paul lifted his hand and pointed to me. "You have been given much, and much will be required of you. Even if you bury many of the talents entrusted to you, you can accomplish far more than others, but you will have failed in your commission. You must never measure yourself by others, but keep pressing forward, seeking more of Him. And yet, with all of the glory that will be revealed to you, never take off that cloak!"

## Sowing and Reaping

I looked down at the cloak of humility to which he was pointing. In all of the glory that I was now seeing, its drabness seemed multiplied. I was appalled that I looked so bad standing in their presence. I drew it back to see the armor under it, which was now more brilliant than I had seen it before. It was so brilliant that the more I uncovered it, the more the group in front of me faded because of its brightness. However, I was feeling far less embarrassed with the brightness of my armor shining out. I then decided to take the cloak all of the way off while I was there so that I would at least not feel as repulsive in the presence of so much glory.

There was silence, and I stood quietly for a few moments. I was unable to see anything because of the brightness of my own armor. I did not understand why I could not hear anything either. I then called out for Wisdom.

*"Put your cloak back on,"* I heard Him reply. I did as He said and began to dimly see the outline of the Great Hall again.

"Lord, what happened to everyone? Why is everything so dim again?"

*"You can see nothing here without wearing that cloak."*

"But I have it on now, and I still cannot see very well," I protested, feeling a terrible desperation.

*"Every time you take off humility you will be blinded to the true light, and it will take time for you to be able to see it again."*

Even though I was beginning to see the glory again, it was nothing like before. My vision was coming back, but very, very slowly. I was grieved beyond words.

"Where is Paul?" I asked. "I know that he was about to tell me something very important."

*"When you took off your cloak, all of those who were here departed."*

"Why? Why would they depart just because I took off the cloak? I was just embarrassed by my appearance. Did that offend them?"

*"No, they were not offended. They knew that you could not see or hear Me through them without the cloak, so they returned to their places."*

I was more grieved than ever at this statement. "Lord, I know that what they were about to say to me was very important. Will they return?"

"*It is true that you missed an important revelation by taking off your cloak. It would have helped you, but if you learn the lesson not to ever take off the cloak again, especially for the reason that you just did, you will have learned another important lesson.*"

"Lord, I think that I have learned that lesson. I do not remember ever feeling this bad. Can they not come back now and share what they had for me?" I begged.

"*All Truth and all Wisdom comes from Me. I speak through people because the people I speak through are a part of the message. While you remained humble enough to keep your cloak on, I could speak to you in glory. Whenever you take off that cloak, you become spiritually blind and deaf. I will always speak to you if you call on Me, but I must change the way that I speak to you.*

"*I do not do this to punish you, but to help you receive your vision back more quickly. I will give you the message that I was going to give you through these witnesses, but it must now be given through your enemies. It will come with trials, and you will have to bow very low to receive it. This is the only way that you will get your vision back as quickly as you will need it. For what is coming, you must be able to see.*"

## Brokenness

The grief I felt was almost unbearable. I knew that what I could have received in such a glorious way was now going to come through great trials, but even worse than that was the fact that the great glory which I had beheld just a few minutes before was now so dim.

"Lord, I am sorry for what I did. I now know how wrong it was. The pain of this mistake is almost too much to bear. Is there no way that I can just be forgiven and receive my vision back? It does not seem right that one brief moment of pride should be this devastating," I pleaded.

*"You are forgiven. Nothing is being done to you for punishment. I paid the price for this sin and all others. You live by My grace. This is not because of the Law of righteousness. It is because of My grace that there are consequences for sin. You must reap what you sow or I could not trust you with My authority. When Satan took his first step into self-seeking and pride, multitudes of My angels who I had entrusted to his authority followed him. When Adam fell, multitudes would suffer. For those to whom I give such authority, there is a corresponding responsibility. There can be no true authority without responsibility. Responsibility does mean that others will suffer if you go astray. Mistakes have consequences.*

*"The more authority you are given, the more that you can either help or hurt others by your actions. To remove the consequences of your actions would be to remove true authority. You are a part of the new creation that is much higher than the first creation. Those who are called to rule with Me are given the greatest responsibility of all. They are called to a position higher than Satan held. He was a great angel, but he was not a son. You are called to be a joint heir*

with Me. Your whole life, both the trials and the revelations, are all for the purpose of teaching you the responsibility of authority.

"For every lesson that you must learn, there is an easy way or a more difficult way. You can humble yourself, fall on the rock and be broken, or the rock will fall on you and crush you into powder. Either way, the final result will be brokenness, which is humility. Pride caused the first fall from grace, and it has caused most of the falls since. Pride always results in tragedy, darkness and suffering. It is for your sake and for those whom you are called to serve by having authority over that I will not compromise the discipline you must learn by reaping what you sow.

"Adonijah boasted that his father, King David, did not discipline him. Solomon complained that he could not get away with anything without his father's discipline. Although Solomon thought that he was not being treated fairly, David was not being unfair. He knew that Solomon was called to be a king. Those who receive the most discipline are those who are called to walk in greater authority.

"You were blinded because you stepped out of humility and began to move in pride. The humble cannot be embarrassed. When you start to feel embarrassed, it is because you are beginning to move in pride. Let the embarrassment be a warning that you have departed from wisdom. Never let embarrassment control your actions. If it does, you will fall even further. Learn to embrace every opportunity *to be humbled, knowing that I will then be able to trust you with more authority.*

*"Do not boast in your strengths, but in your weaknesses. If you will openly talk more about your failures in order to help others, I will be able to more openly display your victories, 'For everyone who exalts himself shall be humbled, and he who humbles himself shall be exalted.'"*

I knew that everything He said was true. I had preached the same message many times. I thought of how Paul had warned Timothy to pay attention to his own teaching and realized that I felt that I needed my messages more than those to whom I preached. Now I was more ashamed by the shining armor I wore than of the humble cloak. I pulled the cloak even tighter. When I did this, my eyes brightened and my vision grew strikingly better, even though it was still far from what it had been.

I turned to see the door. I was afraid to go back through it, at least until I had received more of my vision back.

*"You must go now,"* Wisdom said.

"What is on the other side?" I asked.

*"Your destiny,"* He replied.

I knew that I must go. I was still very sorry that I could not enter the door again with the vision that I had previously because I already knew how dark it was on the other side. I will be even more dependent on others for a time, I thought and committed myself to trusting the Lord and not my own vision. Immediately my eyes grew brighter again. I started to look once more back at the Great Hall to see if they were as bright as they had been, but decided not to. I just determined that it was better now not to look back. Then Wisdom appeared beside me, almost as brilliant as before. My eyes had adjusted to the light so quickly that I could now look at Him. He said nothing, but just looking at Him gave me great courage. Even so, I still felt remorse that I had not heard all of the message I had been about to receive from the cloud of witnesses.

*"If remorse is turned into resolve, the trial will be much easier. Then when your enemies appear to exalt themselves over you, you will grow even more in the authority to prevail over My enemies."*

When I looked back at the door, I was amazed. I saw so much more on it now than I had seen before that for a moment I thought that I was at a different door. It seemed to have grown still more beautiful and was unlike any door I had ever seen, even in this realm. There were exalted titles written in a most beautiful script, all in gold and silver. There were beautiful jewels I did not recognize, but that were so compelling it was difficult to turn my gaze from them. They were all alive. I then realized that the entire door was alive.

As I gazed at the door, Wisdom laid His hand on my shoulder. *"This is the door to My house."* When He said this, I immediately understood that the attraction I now felt for this door was the same that I felt when I looked at Him. It *was* Him somehow. How could anything this beautiful have looked so plain and uninviting before, I pondered. The Lord answered my unspoken question.

*"You cannot see My house as it is until you see Me in My people. As you began to really hear Me through My people just before you took off your cloak, your eyes were opened to begin seeing My house as it is. There is much more glory to be seen in it than you can now behold. This is the door, but there is much more. When you return to the realm of your own time, this is what you must seek. This is what you must lead My people to. This is what you must fight for, and this is what you must help to build—My house."*

With Wisdom's hand upon me, I walked toward the door. It did not open, but I passed right through the midst of it. I do not believe that there is a human language that could describe what I felt as I passed through. I saw the glory of all ages in a single moment. I saw the earth and the heavens as one. I saw myriads of angels, and I saw myriads of people who were more glorious than any angel I had yet seen. These were all serving in His house.

Now I knew the call. Even though I had already been through so much, I knew that my quest was just beginning.

# OTHER BOOKS BY RICK JOYNER

Prophetic Vision for the 21st Century
The Final Quest
The Prophetic Ministry
The Surpassing Greatness of His Power
Epic Battles of the Last Days
There Were Two Trees in the Garden
The Journey Begins
The Harvest
Mobilizing the Army of God
Leadership, Management, and the Five Essentials of Success
The World Aflame
Visions of the Harvest

Combating Spiritual Strongholds Series:
  Overcoming the Accuser
  Overcoming the Spirit of Poverty
  Overcoming Racism
  Overcoming the Religious Spirit
  Overcoming Witchcraft

Hall of Faith Series:
  Three Witnesses
  Courage That Changed the World
  The Fire That Could Not Die